STRADEGY

STR▲DEGY
ADVERTISING IN THE DIGITAL AGE

Dr. Steven J. Fredericks

TNS Media Intelligence
New York, New York

Copyright © 2007 Steven J. Fredericks and TNS Media Intelligence

All rights reserved. No part of this book may be reproduced or transmitted in any form or by any means, electronic or mechanical, including photocopying, recording, or by any information storage and retrieval system, without permission in writing from the publisher.

Published by TNS Media Intelligence
100 Park Avenue
New York, NY 10017

Publisher's Cataloging-in-Publication Data
Fredericks, Steven J., Dr.

StrADegy : Advertising in the Digital Age / Steven J. Fredericks. – New York, NY : TNS Media Intelligence, 2007.

p. ; cm.
ISBN: 0-9788630-0-3
ISBN13: 978-0-9788630-0-5

1. Advertising media planning. 2. Advertising—Research. I. Title.

HF5826.5 .F74 2006
659.1/11—dc22   2006907464

Coordination by Jenkins Group, Inc • www.BookPublishing.com
Interior design by Debbie Sidman
Cover design by Barbara Hodge

Printed in the United States of America
11 10 09 08 07 • 5 4 3 2 1

Dedicated to the memory of Raia Rosenzweig, my dear mother-in-law who always believed in a future of harmony and peace

Contents

Acknowledgments ix

Foreword xi

Chapter One: The New Normal 1

Chapter Two: The Way We Were 15

Chapter Three: Where We Are Today 29

Chapter Four: The Three Futures of Advertising 39

Chapter Five: The Empowered Consumer 53

Chapter Six: Advertising and Politics..................... 67

Chapter Seven: The Future of Agencies.................. 81

Chapter Eight: Digital Transformation and Vertical Industries... 95

Chapter Nine: Law and Order......................... 109

Chapter Ten: The Potential Dark Side 123

Final Thoughts..................................... 137

Notes... 141

ACKNOWLEDGMENTS

Although all authors would like to think that the concepts and ideas contained in their writings all germinated from their own mind, it's mostly a myth. At least for me it is. My thinking has always been an integration of what I see, read, hear, and do—probably no different from most people. Originality requires experience and interaction with the world, and to that end, I am most grateful to my friends, coworkers, and family.

My colleagues at TNS Media Intelligence (TNS-MI), including but not limited to Jean-Michel Portier, Bev Andal, Evan Tracey, Mark Nesbitt, Jon Swallen, Lori Madeloff, Suzie Ross, Carl Dickens, Henry Laura, and Pete Andrel, always challenge me to think clearer and when I go off the deep end are always there to reel me back in. Belene Mallon has ferried this project along from beginning to end and deserves all the credit for keeping me on schedule and focused. Ellen Neuborne brought her incredible insight and experience to the table and was absolutely invaluable to the successful completion of the manuscript. Mark Masarof provided me with "feet on the ground" observations of how the United States lost the textile business because of the industry's inability to cope with the speed and scope of change. It collapsed over a three-year period. The advertising industry would do well to heed those warnings.

To my friends at Peppercom, thank you Steve, Jackie, and your team for all of your positive reinforcement and encouragement. To my industry colleagues, who one way or another were responsible for this foray into tomorrow, I owe you a debt of gratitude. In particular, this book could not have been possible without the ongoing give and take

I have had over the past few years with Nina Link, Ellen Oppenheim, and Wayne Eadie of the Magazine Publishers of America; Jill Manee of *Advertising Age*; Bob Barocci, Diane Streckfuss, and Joe Plummer of the Advertising Research Foundation; TNS-MI Client Advisory Councils; and countless others in the agency and media world who always let me know when I was wrongheaded but were also totally receptive and supportive of some of my ideas that actually made sense.

My family has put up with my intellectual yearnings (and piles of books) for decades now and has always encouraged me in whatever flights of fancy I pursued. This book project was no different. My wife, Luba, is the smartest person I know, and her constant and caring support of my work is all the motivation I need to continue. My son, Justin, contributed his own research on patents as a proxy for innovation while studying at Harvard Law School. It was a brilliant analysis that was quickly integrated into the manuscript, and I continue to worry that I am not doing it justice. During the past three years, my wife and I have been blessed with two grandchildren, Alyssa and Kailey, thanks to my daughter, Dahlia, and her husband, Kevin. They provide me with a joy of life that I have not known since my own children were born. Whenever I need to get energized and ready to take on the next challenge, a visit to see Alyssa and Kailey always sets me off on my way and usually in the right direction. They will be firsthand observers of the veracity of what I had to say here as they enter their teenage years.

The usual disclaimer is that any errors or omissions are mine solely, and I take full responsibility for them. Of course, only the future will tell.

FOREWORD

The future isn't what I expected.

A little more than 30 years ago, I was studying with a professor who claimed he was a futurist. In those days, the notion of an academic futurist was not well understood, especially by me (if I remember it right, I thought he was a little kooky). However, he was on my doctoral committee, so I figured that if he was happy, live and let live. And then I read Alvin Toffler's book *Future Shock*, and I got it.

Toffler spoke about the acceleration of change, and it resonated with me. The problem with change is its nature. Is it random? Is it happening too fast to grasp it? Can you really plan for it, or do you bet your company every time you decide on a course of action to embrace it? Do you run for the hills and cover your head because you yearn for the good old days when you believed the present was your future, life seemed much simpler, and you were content (or convinced yourself that you were)? The real challenge for me, however, was—and still remains to be—how to organize my thinking about change. What constructs can we create that order the world even as we are hurtling toward the future at increasing speed?

That is basically why I decided to write this book. I didn't expect the future we are living in because I thought that change would occur even faster than we are currently experiencing it. I thought that people and institutions were more flexible and less entrenched, that change would be actively embraced, which in turn, would accelerate the change process even further. Arguably, technological advances have far outstripped our ability to keep up with them. I just thought we could. And then I began focusing on why there was this disconnect.

Over the years, as I morphed from one career to another, I was always thinking about the future—but not in the usual sense. I have never formally planned my career. When I came to a crossroad, I always took the fork that appeared more interesting. It may not have been the most practical path to take, but it certainly kept me from getting bored. What I mean by the statement that I was always thinking about the future is that the common thread weaving itself through my professional career was the notion of "future think."

So, when I taught elementary school in the South Bronx (I was born and raised within walking distance of where I taught), the only hope I could hold out for my students was a future that could present itself with opportunities that the present had denied them. When I moved on to the chairmanship of a graduate school department, I taught seminars on "Ethics and the Politics of Education," where we struggled with trying to describe the ideal ethical political system. Of course, by then I had been influenced by writings as diverse as Robert Pirsig's *Zen and the Art of Motorcycle Maintenance* and Paulo Freire's *Pedagogy of the Oppressed* (it was the '70s, after all). So the practicality of much of the thinking was totally debatable. Yet at least we were thinking.

And then, of all things, I left for an extended period to work for IBM. Totally incongruous but, as I said before, interesting. At IBM I always was thinking about the future. In many ways, we were inventing the future, and it was exciting in a virtual context. Although the world was changing rapidly and I was in the middle of perhaps the greatest technological enterprise the world had ever seen, it was still somewhat elusive to me personally. The future was becoming much more complicated than I had anticipated. As a result, when the opportunity arose to focus on a smaller vision of the future, I ran with it.

Digital Domain became my home for a number of years, and we created images that the world had never experienced before. I was in the movie business! That's when I started thinking seriously about the digital future. It was in Venice, California, among the tattoos and body piercings, where we were deeply engaged in the concepts of digital convergence. The technology we created would become recognized as groundbreaking. We created images on the big screen (*Titanic* and *Apollo 13*, to name a few) that came as close to representing visual realities as anyone had ever seen before. We were working toward creating the virtual actor, and each day we were coming closer to realizing that goal. We were helping to define the future. We weren't struggling with it; we embraced it.

There are many documented cases of industries and business areas within those industries experiencing difficult periods in which change was swirling around them. Some survived, and some did not. Sometimes they chose to ignore the realities, sometimes they acted but acted too late, and sometimes they survived because they met the challenges and viewed those challenges as opportunities—which brings me to the advertising industry. Soon after I joined TNS Media Intelligence, it became painfully obvious to me that the advertising industry was trying to act, but was coming a little late to the party. Why? My take is that the industry was really confused. It was confused because there were so many fundamental questions being raised about the relevance and applicability of the industry methods and practices as it entered the digital age. These questions could not be easily answered without a construct of how to think about the digital world. And of course, there always existed, and continues to exist, an overarching silo mentality: "my medium is better than yours." Now, I didn't come to this conclusion overnight. However, after spending a number of years attending the conferences, reading the research, and listening to the interminable debates on the same subjects, you eventually do reach the point where it appears that the industry has basically been focused on rearranging the deck chairs. I was growing tired of it, as have many of my colleagues throughout the industry.

My frustration with the status quo focused my thinking even further. It was an Advertising Research Foundation workshop where interested professionals from the media, advertising agencies, advertisers, and research organizations gathered to discuss the possibilities for the future that the idea for this book, a stake in the ground if you will, started to take form. My intention is to stir the pot, to incite debate, but most important, to actively embrace the future knowing that although there are sure to be many risks, bad assumptions, and even some stupidity, unless we engage it, we will be left behind because the train is certainly leaving the station. I'm jumping on the train and invite you to be my fellow passengers.

One

The New Normal

There's a popular story making the rounds of advertising conference panels. The tale—perhaps apocryphal, certainly illustrative—paints a startlingly clear picture of what the ad industry and its players now face.

It goes like this:

> The following is the transcription of a radio conversation between a U.S. Navy vessel and Canadian authorities off the coast of Newfoundland in the fall of 1995.
>
> Canadians: Please change your course 15 degrees to the south to avoid collision.
>
> Americans: Recommend you change your course 15 degrees to the north to avoid collision.
>
> Canadians: Negative. You will have to change your course 15 degrees to the south to avoid collision.
>
> Americans: This is the captain of a U.S. Navy ship. I say, again, change your course.
>
> Canadians: No. I say, again, change your course.
>
> Americans: This is the aircraft carrier USS *Lincoln*, the second largest ship in the U.S. Atlantic fleet. We are accompanied by three destroyers, three cruisers, and numerous support vessels. I demand you change your course 15 degrees to the north.
>
> Canadians: This is a lighthouse. Your call.

The story generally gets an appreciative laugh. But more than a pleasant introduction to a speech, the story serves another, more critical, purpose. It is an apt description of the advertising industry today. We are, without a doubt, the USS *Lincoln*, a bold, powerful, successful collection of firepower, steaming ahead through familiar waters. And we are bearing down on something, something big, something in our path, something that will require that we alter course and adjust our progress. What is the obstacle ahead? And how should we respond? This book will address those questions.

The first is actually relatively easy. The object ahead has a name: it is digital transformation. That is the seismic event that has recalibrated the business universe and placed its impact directly in the path of the advertising world. And like the lighthouse in the anecdote, there's no waving it off. It is fixed, and it is huge. It is at the core of every trend buffeting the industry today.

It is a product well defined by its brand name. At its root, the digital transformation is a revolution of technology. Just as fossil fuel propelled the massive cultural and economic shifts of the industrial revolution, the digital construct is the driving force of change in our era. Change comes in our time in the form of ones and zeroes. It comes in square screens that sit eye level on our desks, it comes in video we watch on our cell phones, and it comes in harnesses we apply to the wide-open landscape of broadcast entertainment. Whatever is new or different or attractive to us today takes digital form and claims digital ancestry. It frames our lives and propels our era of change.

But more than just technological, the object ahead is transformative. That's an important concept to embrace. This is not a shift, not a blip, not new and improved. The change we are experiencing now is on a more profound level. It not only changes our present experience but also rewrites our history and recalibrates our future path. The final leap over the line is what nails the importance of our experience and its impact on our industry going forward.

So instead of debating tactics—Is the 30-second spot dead? Is paid search for real? Does my brand need a blog?—savvy marketers need to look more broadly at the digital transformation and its impact on the industry.

The digital transformation can be viewed in five distinct parts: acceleration, fragmentation, convergence, empowerment, and permanence. By understanding the role each of these pillars plays in the transformative experience, marketers can better predict the future of a digitally transformed marketplace.

ACCELERATION

A hallmark of digital transformation is the speed at which it happens. Experience is compressed and rapid-fired through business and social cycles. The rate of acceleration impacts not only the velocity at which events happen but also the way we process them, affecting how we feel, communicate, and create.

The speed at which human invention moves has accelerated radically in just a few lifetimes. The forward clip has snowballed and will continue to gain momentum, thus making swift adaptation a cornerstone of success. The significance of the speed of change cannot be underestimated. In his landmark work *Future Shock*, Alvin Toffler examined the accelerating nature of change in human life:

> "If the last 50,000 years of man's existence were divided into lifetimes of approximately 62 years each, there have been about 800 such lifetimes. Of these 800, 650 were spent in caves. Only during the last 70 lifetimes has it been possible to communicate effectively from one lifetime to another—as writing made it possible to do. Only during the last six lifetimes did masses of people ever see a printed word. Only during the last four has it been possible to measure time with any precision. Only in the last two has anyone anywhere used an electric motor. And the overwhelming majority of all material goods we use in daily life today have been developed within the present, the 800th, lifetime."[1]

In our own era, the acceleration of technological change has been palpable, reworking human experience on a regular basis and with dizzying results. Technological advance, science tells us, is exponential. In the twenty-first century, we won't experience 100 years of progress. Instead, understanding the avalanche rate at which technology morphs, we can expect 20,000 years of progress at today's rate. That spectacular projection is fathomable when one looks around at just the most recent technological upgrades and their seismic impacts. Take, for example, broadband or the World Wide Web or nanotechnology. All were elements of science fiction within our lifetimes. Now, they are not only a reality but also, for many, an everyday occurrence.

The speed at which technology leaps from drawing boards to living rooms is faster than it's ever been, and it is gaining velocity with each incarnation. Futurist Ray Kurzweil calls the process the "Law of Accelerating Returns" and predicts that within a few decades—certainly in the parameters of the current eight-hundredth lifetime—technological change will zoom ahead with such ferocity that it will rupture the fabric of human intellectual capacity and necessitate technological help—true artificial intelligence—to understand and process the world.

To be sure, the advertising industry has experienced this accelerating change. Where there were once a handful of outlets for communicating with consumers, there are now dozens, and there are more possibilities and permutations every day. A generation of admen spent their careers pondering the palate of television, print, and radio. But today's communicators face new distribution platforms, such as the Internet and the cell phone. Housed within these new platforms are dozens of new formats, such as e-mail, search, banners, buttons, blogs, webcasts, podcasts, and Real Simple Syndication (RSS). New incarnations emerge 24/7. The rate of change has spun the industry around, forcing it to abandon assumptions, hauling it forcibly into a state of constant technological change—of digital transformation.

A final word on acceleration: it rarely reverses. In the history of technological innovation, there has rarely been a successful invention that slowed a process down. Indeed, technological change is married to the idea of speed itself. So while the speed of change may be breathtaking, challenging, and even maddening, it is the reality of the digitally transformed space.

FRAGMENTATION

It's 10 p.m. Do you know where your consumers are?

Just a few years ago, that was an easy question. At 10 p.m., the most attractive consumers were more than likely sitting in front of the television and were watching the last hour of prime-time programming. But that was then, before fragmentation.

Audience fragmentation is the outcome of the digital transformation that has most immediately affected the advertising industry. It began with the evolution of television to cable television and then to digital cable and to satellite. As the platforms expanded, the offerings narrowed. Movie channels led to genre movie channels with specialty themes—Westerns, romances, sci-fis, and thrillers. Sports channels gave rise to single sports channels and then even to team-specific channels. Audiences once content to sit for a mass-market offering now pealed off in droves to enjoy the more targeted fare.

Television was not the only medium affected. Magazines experienced the breakup, with titles such as *Life* giving way to *Cottage Living* and *Cigar Aficionado*. Even the Internet, a driving force of fragmentation in other media, experienced the combustion. While the space was early on dominated by its own mass-market brands—AOL, Microsoft, Yahoo!—today a fragmented Internet means that sites are constructed not for the mass, or even for the niche, but right down to the individual. The entire online space has fragmented into one-to-one conversations. No communication platform is sheltered from the impact. Every consumer point of contact can be split and its pieces redistributed. The offerings have only expanded. At 10 p.m. today, your once rock-solid audience may be scattered across multiple platforms and entertainment options. And fragmentation is a trend that continues to feed upon itself. Says David Schatsky of Jupiter Research:

> "Media itself is beginning to fragment in dramatic ways. Individual songs and episodes of TV series are available for sale via download. Digital 'feeds' of newspaper and magazine content allow consumers to read parts of a publication out of context without ever seeing the rest. Cable companies may soon offer individual channels a la carte. Consumers increasingly expect to be able to consume media when and where they want, on any platform or device, in any context. The technology and media industries are beginning to oblige them. Fragmentation is both a cause and effect, creating a cycle in which fragmented audiences lead to fragmented content, which allows audiences to fragment further, and so on."[2]

On the one hand, this evolution has a tremendous upside. For any advertiser who was ever daunted by the expense of cracking the mass market, fragmentation is a gift. No longer must a company marshal the resources to tackle network television or major-league sponsorship. Indeed, the road to success now has many more access ramps. The selection is plentiful, driving the cost down and the possibilities up. Many more messages, of new products and services, of new ideas, of far-flung voices, will have their moment. That was once possible only for the best-connected and the best-financed of the pack. Fragmentation allows many more ideas to pile on to the commercial stage.

Consumers, too, benefit from the fragmentation process. In addition to the benefit of hearing new ideas, fragmentation goes a long way toward improving the individual experience of and relationship with media and messaging. Instead of sitting through information and entertainment with little or no relevance, individuals can now tailor their choices with more precision, and they expect marketers to be similarly focused on their wants and needs. The splinter process allows consumers to enjoy more of what they like and less of what they don't. While this entertains and informs, it goes one step further and strengthens the bonds between consumers and media. As communication becomes more relevant, more targeted, and more personal, individual consumers become more attached to it. It positions media as a life element on the upswing, improving in performance rather than remaining stagnant.

Near-term wrestling with the reality of fragmentation is no easy task, despite all its benefits in the long run. The ad industry must take the shattered landscape as both a blessing and a curse. Opportunities abound thanks to it. But they are opportunities for both success and failure. For every great message that managed to reach its audience through the fragmented array of television, magazines, newspapers, or radio, there are others that slipped off into unwatched, unnoticed oblivion. Choosing from among the many fragments is the new core competency of the skilled advertiser. But the newness of the space means there is little precedent to follow. In an array of 500+ channels, where are the eyeballs your marketer most wants to reach? And even if you've found the perfect niche platform, does that mean your target consumers will be there to receive your message? The uncertainty of the fragmented media world is pervasive. Networks were predictable. This new breed of niche media has no history to guide it, no set path to follow. The ad industry must strive to make a usable picture of the puzzle pieces.

CONVERGENCE

If the era has a buzzword, it is "convergence." It is the fusion that emerges from the vast assortment of fragmentation. Puzzle pieces break from their original borders and make new connections, new platforms, new possibilities.

Still, convergence isn't a new concept. Communications scholar Ithiel de Sola Pool in his 1983 book *The Technologies of Freedom* helped give the concept its first boost into popular consciousness:

"The explanation for the current convergence between historically separated modes of communication lies in the ability of digital electronics. Conversation, theater, news and text are all increasingly delivered electronically ... Electronic technology is bringing all modes of communications into one grand system."[3]

It took a while, but the concept caught on. In the early '90s, we all talked about convergence. The television, the PC, and the telephone would converge into one handy delivery device. We marked our calendars for about 1997, and companies—especially software developers—poured millions into development. Turns out hardware convergence took a little longer to percolate than originally predicted. It's only now—about 10 years late by some estimations—that the devices are emerging. But emerging they are: computers that support television, televisions that access the Web, e-mail devices that play music, phones that do all of those things plus take your picture. Device convergence is upon us.

Advertising has had to adapt quickly to this converged environment. Once clearly-drawn delineating lines have quickly blurred. The multitalented devices mean a convergence of message distribution. Consumers don't care whether you've made a TV spot or a radio commercial. They want to access it on demand, from whatever device they've got handy. The notion that a message might be available on only one device is, well, so 1997. Digital transformation has left that practice in the technological dust.

From hardware, the convergence trend has further evolved to bring fusion to other areas of consumer experience. Cultural activities are blended—bringing us infotainment, edutainment, and other mixed messaging once delivered in carefully separated silos. As those lines blur, business is finding other converged platforms on which to reach consumers. Consider the rise of branded entertainment—the convergence of advertising and content. Marketers look at more than just the commercial breaks, including the full TV experience as a forum for brand marketing messages. Once on the sidelines, brands are now in the story line, and companies measure for the type and prominence of each brand appearance recorded, including visual and verbal dimensions, character interaction, time duration, brand visibility and exclusivity, and level of plot integration. Once-separate entities have converged, an outcome of the digital transformation of the industries.

Convergence offers many benefits to consumers and marketers, but it is not without its challenges—perhaps the greatest of which is that it is not a fixed state of being. As new alliances are formed, others dissolve. It is a continuous loop of marriage, dissolution, and reconnection. But even as the partners may shift and swap, the message to advertising is consistent: be ready for the next incarnation. As digital transformation breaks apart old connections and allows new ones to form, the mission of the industry will be to communicate under any and all circumstances.

EMPOWERMENT

Once upon a time, the advertising industry delivered a steady stream of carefully researched messaging to a waiting mass market. Digital transformation turned that relationship on its head. In the modern era, consumers wait for no message. Ads happen on consumer terms, on consumer timetables, and in consumer control. It is a complete reversal of the industry's history.

It began innocently enough, with the ability to change channels on the TV set without getting up. "Surfing" during commercial breaks became a common activity. Family members squabbled over the right to hold the "clicker" and engage in this exercise of control over media. And it was only the beginning. Then, VCRs allowed viewers to fast-forward through commercials, and then, DVRs offered yet a new level of consumer control: ad skipping. And there's every indication that more ad avoidance technology is in the works. It is certainly possible that soon—in a matter of years—consumers will be fully in control of the ads they see and hear. Certainly, through each incarnation thus far, consumers have made their intentions clear: they want ads when they want them, on their own schedules. Says Alan Moore, coauthor of *Communities Dominate Brands*:

> "History has shown, once you have stormed the Bastille, you don't go back to your day jobs. And the empowered consumer is not going to give the Bastille back—and why should they?"[4]

This is not to say that empowered consumers do not want to view advertising. Indeed, millions of consumers volunteer for ad messages all the time. In doctor's offices, thousands of new moms sign up every year to receive direct marketing pitches and samples from child care consumer products companies. Teens eagerly hand over their e-mail addresses to the handlers of their favorite bands or celebrities for news of the latest wares for sale. Super Bowl parties hush during commercial breaks so that guests can enjoy the latest creative from Anheuser-Busch. Consumers are not anti-advertising; they are simply anti-passivity. They're just not willing to sit back and let advertising wash over them in the old-fashioned, mass-market manner. Instead, they want to participate in the distribution process of advertising. Indeed, they insist. And technology now says they can.

The digital transformation has created empowered consumers—consumers with the ability to control when and where advertising happens. And that power continues to expand. Thanks to new and improved technology, consumers do more than just view advertising on demand. They can create it. Internet sites have sprung up that encourage visitors to create and post their own ads. Consumers logged on to craft their own pitches for Burger King featuring the burger chain's surreal masked mascot. The resulting content drew millions of virtual viewers. Empowered consumers are hardly against advertising. Indeed, they are willing to lend a hand and be part of the ad process. That's the power of digital transformation in consumers' hands.

But the newly empowered consumers also pose a serious challenge to the industry—one from which the industry can't hide. Because consumers have new blocking power, advertising has to be good advertising. Bad ads, lazy ads, and irrelevant ads will simply fail and die a lonely death in unwatched oblivion. In the old days, everyone in front of the television watched ads. Those days are over. If you want your ad viewed, it'd better be good. If it's not, empowered consumers are under no obligation to sit still for it.

PERMANENCE

The digital transformation is not a fad. It is not a trend. It is not a temporary state of flux. It is the new normal. It is life as we know it. It is permanent. That's not news. Says Vinton Cerf, who jointly developed the TCP/IP protocol on which the Internet is based, "You can't stop technology. It just doesn't work. So you have to figure out how to live with it."[5]

Need proof of the permanency of digital transformation? You probably have it on your person right now. Take out your cell phone. Think about how often you use it. If you're like most business executives, it's a minimum of 10 times per day. Now, think back to when you didn't have a cell phone. Again, for most, that would be anywhere from five to 10 years ago. That was when checking in with the office required a pay phone, when checking messages meant sorting through a stack of pink paper slips, when news of home and family had to wait until after office hours.

In those intervening years, individuals experienced digital transformation. It's the experience by which a technological advance moves into individuals' lives and reworks basic assumptions. For the cell phone, the speed and mobility of communication reworked notions of connectivity, conversation, and connection. It was not simply a new technology; it was a transformative experience.

Now, test the permanence of your transformation. Imagine if you were approached and told you had to give up your cell phone and go back to the old days. How would you react? The latest research in workplace behavior suggests that executives would give up every single office device—from the fax to the copier to the coffeemaker—before parting with the cell phone. It's that integral to the daily business experience. It's here to stay. Digital transformation complete. The effect is permanent. There's little chance anyone using a cell phone today would be willing to go back to pink "while you were out" slips. We have experienced a digital transformation, and we are not going back.

That's a crucial reality for the industry to face. Far too many players think they are simply waiting out an era of flux and change that will sort itself out and return to "normal." Change, in this era, is a constant, forward-moving experience. Just as shouting at the lighthouse to move is futile, so too is holding still and waiting for the era of change to pass.

These five themes make up the challenge and the opportunity facing the industry.

So now, understanding what is ahead of us, what do we do about it? This is the more complicated question, and it is the one we'll address throughout the rest of this book. But here is a starting point: rise above the tactical debate.

The ad industry and its interested parties are spending time and money to debate the future of television, the relevance of print, the potential of e-mail, and the wisdom of search. All are valid conversations. But they are not going to generate the road map through this era of change. The solution is not to pick "the" tactic. Instead, the answer is to craft a strategy that is tactic neutral, one that works on a broader level and is not married to any one delivery system.

Consider this: all ad messaging today falls into one of three categories. No matter where or how you find an ad, it will be one of these three: text, video, or audio. To date, there is no other configuration.

There might be one day, but for now, these are our three vessels. Your ad strategy will likely use all of these, individually or in combination, at all times.

There is no need—indeed, there is no excuse—for choosing just one. These are the three elements in which consumers receive information. Use all three, and tailor your message to each. If your pitch is text, audio, and video ready, it will rise above the daily chatter. It won't matter whether your screen is big or small, whether your music is satellite or broadcast, whether your print is newspaper or blog. Video, audio, text. Three compartments. One system. No tactical debate.

Critical to that system is the quality of the ad message. In an era marked by speed, fragmentation, technical convergence, and empowered consumers, there is no room for lazy advertising. Message and market must be laser targeted. This is not an era that will suffer flab.

There is indeed an object ahead of us. It is the reality of digital transformation. It will not move off and clear a path for us. The charge is on us to change course. The plan of action: adjust to its realities, embrace the change it has brought, and keep focus on the core elements of the ad conversation. Throughout the rest of this book, we'll examine the state of the industry, the possibilities for its future, and what change digital transformation has already brought to key players in our space. Through this examination, we'll begin to see a clear view of the future of advertising.

Two

The Way We Were

Consider the following quote and see whether you can place it in time:

> " ... the whole world was worried and overworked and perplexed by problems that would not get stated simply, that changed and evaded solution, it was in an atmosphere that had corrupted and thickened past breathing; there was no thorough cool thinking in the world at all. There was nothing ... anywhere but half-truths, hasty assumptions, hallucinations, and emotions. Nothing ..."[1]

It's targeted enough to be modern commentary, but in fact, it's H. G. Wells, circa 1906. While the words were written long ago, the message is one for our times: change and challenge come in every era. It looks easy only in hindsight.

It's natural to look back with rose-colored glasses, back at simpler times, gentler times. In an era of change and challenge, the old days look plain, attractive, even idyllic. Faced today with shifting technology, consumer demands, and an uncertain future, it's easy to see why the past takes on a certain aura of nostalgia and desirability.

But the days gone by were not so simple to those who lived them. A look back at the history of modern advertising shows companies, technologists, and ad agencies locked in their own battles of the era, wrestling with their own monsters, struggling to make sense of the world ahead.

But looking backward has more than just nostalgic advantages. History provides us with more than just a good tale; it tells how problems we face today have been worked out before. And advertising is no exception. The modern advertising era was born with the advent of broadcast technology, and as it arrived, made its way through the popular consciousness, and changed the relationship between business and consumer, the modern ad era was born.

RADIO DAYS

The technology that brought the audio experience out of the live audience and into the broad consumer marketplace was not born as an ad vehicle. In fact, it wasn't viewed as a true entertainment vehicle in its early incarnation. But as it emerged from a purely technical tool to a consumer product, its image shifted a bit with the times. In the early part of the twentieth century, as more homes had access to a radio, the device found its place in public discourse. Still, it was considered a product of serious purpose. It was used to disseminate information and education. Entertainment at this time was still very much a live experience. It was an in-person event. Remote entertainment was not yet in full swing. And the notion of ad-sponsored content was a crazy idea, often met with contempt and derision by the business elite.

Times began to change in the 1920s—the boom era of radio. During this decade, media met a technological crossroads. The ownership of radio was expanding and so was the breadth of its offerings. Westinghouse established four well-financed stations. The Department of Commerce issued formal regulations establishing broadcast service. And with lightning speed, the radio landscape exploded. By 1922, there were 500 stations broadcasting in the United States, and content followed: news, music, poetry, and even children's programming hit the newly fashioned airwaves.[2]

But the simultaneous transmission of audio content to multiple locations lacked an important element: a profitable business model. Audiences were thrilled with the new experience, but broadcasters pondered the future of this technology: who would pay?

This editorial appeared in the December 1922 edition of *Popular Radio*:

> "The broadcasting crisis in a nutshell: Upon the nature of the broadcast programs the public interest in radio—and consequently the immediate future of the radio industry—is hanging.
>
> "When radio first seized upon the public fancy, interest was centered on the radio apparatus itself—the mechanical medium by which the broadcast programs were received. The novelty of the instrument must inevitably pass. The public's interest is properly becoming centered on the programs themselves.
>
> "Radio is unquestionably destined to play a vital part in the affairs of men, perhaps a more vital part than has ever been played by a single invention or discovery. It is vastly more than a mere instrument for receiving jazz, bed-time stories and similar light entertainment. It has already demonstrated its significance as a great educational and cultural force. The foremost educators and publicists of the country are beginning to realize its possibilities. Radio is beginning to take its place as an instrument for rendering a world-wide public service of inestimable value.
>
> "The day when eminent musicians, lecturers and others can be induced, to visit remote broadcasting stations and entertain free of charge is passing."[3]

Replace the word "radio" with the word "Internet" in the above passage to see just how neatly history repeats itself.

Industry wrestled with its radio problem. A writer for *Popular Science* at the time suggested that radio signals be scrambled and consumers use a coin-operated device to receive programming. It was the early ancestor of pay-per-view television. But it did not catch on with serious purpose in the radio world. The system was already considered too vast for such controls.

It was American Telephone and Telegraph that proposed the solution that would revolutionize advertising: the company called it "toll broadcasting." AT&T would keep radio programming on the air—and sell some of that airtime to marketers to cover the costs.

Response to the idea was swift and negative. Then Commerce Secretary Herbert Hoover said at the National Conference on Radio Telephony, "It is inconceivable that we should allow so great a possibility for service to be drowned in advertising chatter." At a later conference, he was even stronger in his critique, saying, "If the speech by the President is to be used as the meat in the sandwich of two patent medicine advertisements, there will be no radio left."[4]

Even some major broadcasters thought it sounded like a terrible idea. Wrote J. C. McQuiston, manager of the Department of Publicity for Westinghouse, in *Radio News*, August 1922:

> "Let me ask you whether the public will wish advertising to come to them through the agency of radio broadcasting. Remember that this advertising will go right into the home. It will invade the place where the family is enjoying the full benefits of privacy and detachment from business cares. The broadcasting to thousands of homes of advertising information concerning, say: 'Things for women and things for men,' probably the butcher with his meats; the baker with his bread; the tailor with his clothes, and the grocer with his crackers and cheese—what kind of a home will it be anyhow? You may say you can turn it on at will and turn it off when you want to, but even so, who will want it? How valuable will be the media if the public will not support it? Personally, I don't think they will support it."[5]

Early efforts were not well met. Broadcasts by the DeForest Radio Telephone & Telegraph Company's "Highbridge Station," 2XG in New York City, became one of the first to include ads. Its airtime included announcements about products sold by the station owner. But the practice quickly ended when Lee DeForest was embarrassed by industry criticism of his experiment. Indeed, for the rest of his career, he was a vocal critic of the practice, even promoting a remote-control device for silencing radio commercials.[6]

So the era of radio advertising was off to a slow start. Certainly, advertisers had other options. Print continued to grow and evolve during this period. John Wanamaker had made popular the art of the full-page newspaper ad, and retailers had made that form of advertising a regular practice. Print was also a key purveyor of advertising and information on household goods—campaigns pitching cleansers, baking goods, medicinal remedies, and new appliances often took this form to reach the American housewife. This was also the period in which magazines began to move into mass circulation. Titles such as *Life* hit the stands and would go on to carry hundreds of millions in advertising.

But companies would be compelled to reach beyond the traditional print ad format to other means, thanks in part to a major historical event: the Great Depression. During the 1920s, the economy boomed, and American business took credit for the great surge forward in consumer experience. Then came the stock market crash of '29 and the ensuing economic tumble into the Depression Era. And with that change in fortune came a shift in image for American business. The public image of an American corporation shifted from industry titan to soulless leviathan. Industry wasn't collecting accolades—it was taking the blame. Corporate leaders were slow to pick up on this change in their public image and the level of consumer anger that fueled it. In 1931, the head of the National Association of Manufacturers called the Depression "psychological."[7]

By the 1930s, business was beginning to recognize its public relations predicament. Public opinion polls showed that consumers viewed big business with tremendous skepticism and thought it to be of little help in those trying times. Government, on the other hand, was getting a boost in public consciousness. The sweeping victory of Franklin D. Roosevelt in 1936 cemented the realization that consumer trust had been shifted to the public sector. The American corporation was the bad guy.

Ad agency executives watched this shift in fortunes with interest, and a pattern emerged. The rise of FDR had been cemented with the help of a particular medium: radio. In essence, FDR had used radio to communicate his message and his brand essence and to win support and loyalty from the listening public. It was a strategy he used effectively throughout his campaign and presidency. Ad agencies began to form a game plan for business. They began to see a process that could be adapted for their own clients. The plan was to borrow from FDR's playbook and use radio in a way yet untried by American business. They proposed a novel idea: in order to climb out of this hole and reestablish good relations with the American public, American business should forge ahead into the new territory of ad-sponsored radio.

The first radio ads were excruciatingly careful in their attempts to sell without offending. One, a 15-minute talk promoting a New York City apartment complex, was among the first to air. AT&T rejected many other comers for fear of backlash from listeners and government regulators. But the practice caught on, and business gained confidence, built steam, and created the early connection between entertainment and commercials.[8]

After some initial fits and starts, radio advertising caught on with consumers and companies in the form of episodic programming. One of the most famous came from DuPont, a massive company struggling to shrug off its image as a "merchant of death" for its sale of munitions. DuPont invested in the production and broadcast of *Cavalcade of America*, an episodic drama that related tales of American progress, persistence, and ingenuity from the country's history. The half-hour radio plays featured such tales as the arrival of the pilgrims, the building of the Union Pacific railroad, and the establishment of the American Red Cross. Each tale of heroism and true grit was carefully sponsored by DuPont and its tagline "Better living—through chemistry."[9] The show was a hit—and so was its business model. American industry had invented the marriage of advertising and entertainment.

By 1950, American industry had successfully rehabilitated its image with the consuming public, and sponsored content was the norm of the entertainment industry. Now, the stage had been set for the advertising industry to meet its next technological challenge: television.

TV TIME

Television advertising was technically born in 1941.[10] That's when the Federal Communications Commission lifted the ban on commercials and officially declared the end of television's experimental phase. But there was no immediate rush to the new medium from America's marketers. Most of the cutting-edge ad work was still going on in radio. And while millions of radio listeners could be counted across the United States, TV ownership was still quite small. Marketers were uncertain whether television could deliver any meaningful pump to their bottom line. In his book on the early days of television, *Please Stand By*, author Michael Ritchie recounted a salesman's involvement in the pioneering efforts of TV commercials. Pitching one of his best clients, an Ohio beer producer, the salesman was sure he was going to make his very first sale. But in the end, the client turned to him and told him the new medium just didn't seem to be better than his current ad tactic: painting on the side of a barn.[11]

Some brave souls were enticed to test the new waters. Bulova Watch Company paid an estimated $7 to have its timepiece showcased sans voice-over. Procter and Gamble, Lever, and Sun Oil also made early forays. But even at the bargain cost of $100 (production and airtime included), the ad buy got the marketers only about 5,000 homes in New York City. Reach was still not part of the TV promise.[12]

But in its second decade, TV advertising exploded. The spread of the technology itself created a burgeoning consumer market. By the early 1950s, there were more than 16 million sets in American living rooms, each drawing an average of three people to the screen every day. Ad agencies led the march. By 1950, agency giant BBDO had convinced 40 of its clients to advertise on television. The ad shop itself was producing dozens of TV ads per month, half filmed, half live. Spots that would live in advertising history, like those for Lucky Strike cigarettes, were born. By 1955, spending on TV advertising had surpassed that of radio and print.[13]

The road to TV ad success was bumpy. Technical difficulties were regular occurrences. In live ads, it was not unheard of to have an actor flub and use the brand name of a competitor. Products used in demonstrations would sometimes fail to perform on cue. And the hot lights and other harsh conditions of TV studios at the time made ad production a dicey experience. Actors and technicians had to deal with spoiled food, perspiring actors, and, on more than one occasion, an actual fire.

What's more is that as the medium grew, so did the cost of advertising. The entire process was expensive, says Lawrence Samuel, author of *Brought to You By: Postwar Television Advertising and the American Dream*. Television required five times the number of technicians as radio. Marketers were paying as much as $15,000 a week to sponsor variety programs in the late '40s. In 1952, CBS charged $90,000 a week for the sponsorship of *The Jackie Gleason Show*. NBC's *Your Show of Shows* was drawing $1 million for a year's worth of one-minute commercials.[14]

Print remained a steady advertising option. In the 1950s, newspaper readership was still widespread. Historical data from *Editor and Publisher* showed 1.23 newspapers were purchased per household in 1950. The printed page was still a primary source of information and a reliable vehicle for advertising.[15]

But the allure of the new medium was powerful. To adjust to the expense, marketers and their ad strategists made two critical shifts that would set up the boundaries of the modern ad industry. First, the burden of entertainment production was firmly and definitively shifted to the networks. The old days of radio, in which ad agencies wrote both the scripts and the ad copy for their clients, faded away. Additionally, companies began moving away from acting as the sole sponsor of a show and instead were content to buy slices of commercial time—thus spreading the cost of a show over the budgets of more than one eager marketer.

The new medium proved to be a creative springboard for the advertising industry. Freed to use a variety of visual effects, those in the ad industry churned out ads as engaging and entertaining as the shows they sponsored. Dodge ads featured talking bunnies. Animation mixed with live action was used to sell apple cider. Hurdles, such as labor disputes that kept live orchestras off the air, inspired ad makers to find creative solutions that became hallmarks of the industry, such as the a cappella ad jingle and the use of unusual (and non-union) instruments such as the ukulele. Despite the creation of separate commercial breaks, pitchmen were still often woven into the content of the entertainment. Sportscasters casually discussed the benefits of sponsor products during game broadcasts. Jack Benny and other entertainers voiced ad messages during their shows.

Ultimately, companies flocked to television not just for the audience or for the technological excitement of it; they came because TV advertising produced sales. Kraft executives said they rated the success of the sponsorship of the Kraft Television Theater not by ratings but by recipe requests. Kraft products such as McLaren's Imperial Cheese became hits in the grocer's aisle after being featured on the show. Other products and brands, such as Volkswagen, General Electric, and Ivory Soap, counted television as their sales driver.

But while ad formats evolved and the relationship between content and commercial was recast, the most lasting impact of advertising during this early TV era was societal. It was the point at which advertising evolved from a message about goods and services into its own cultural phenomenon.

"Within this relatively short period of time, a new, original culture would form and be canonized in literature, film, and television itself. Most important, television advertising emerged as a loud, and I believe the loudest, voice of the American Dream, promoting the values of consumption and leisure grounded in a domestic, family-oriented lifestyle," wrote Lawrence Samuel.[16]

It was a societal status that holds true half a century later.

Day in the Life of a Consumer: 1955

In the golden age of television, the consumer whom marketers coveted was the American homemaker. She was the user and beneficiary of many of the nation's newest products, and it was her life into which marketers hoped to enter. She had more disposable income than her mother, she had more time to consider leisure, and, surprisingly, she did just as much if not more housework than her predecessors. She was the central worshiper in what ad scholars called the "cult of cleanliness" that sprung up in the decade, dictating a generation of purchasing habits. Here's how her ad day may have progressed:

Morning: The print ads in the morning's newspaper pitched the latest in household necessities, with a twist of the times. Refrigeration had been available to consumers for years, and print ads would reflect the shift in priorities. No longer did the American homemaker have to be sold on the concept of refrigeration for food safety. Now the pitch had evolved: ads of the time offered quality of life. More room for food storage meant less time shopping, less hassle for the lady of the house, more time for leisure activities. Ads for other home appliances would make a similarly suburban paradise pitch. Sewing machines were marketed as fashion tools. Dishwashers were desirable to avoid the dreaded state of "dishpan hands."

Noon: Soap operas made their way into the afternoons of the American homemaker, first as radio dramas and then as some of the longest-running and most popular shows on television. In 1952, *Guiding Light* made its move from radio to television and hasn't been off the air since. True to their moniker, soap operas were ad platforms for the household products of the day. Many were commodities, and that called for a strong dose of product differentiation. Tide countered hard water. Dash was stronger. Ivory Flakes were gentler.

Television and radio were not the only sources of pitches in this time slot. Door-to-door sales were all the rage, and the lady of the house might take a call from a Hoover rep or another traveling peddler.

Night: Evening television evolved into a prime pitch period for the American homemaker. Some shows were developed specifically to court her. The Kraft Home Theater featured dramatic stories that were interspersed with how-to ads for Kraft products. The camera focused on a pair of female hands preparing a dish using Kraft ingredients while voice-over talent read the recipe.

Straightforward commercial breaks were not the only way a woman could be reached during this time slot. As the popularity of television exploded, sports broadcasts discovered for the first time that they could successfully court a female audience. Women who had never been to a live sporting event would be one of the average three people sitting in front of the family television during the broadcast of a game. That meant the popular "ad-lib" advertising, in which the sportscaster would casually drop the brand name of the sponsor into his conversation, extended to household goods.

By the time she retired for the evening, the American homemaker had been courted by a multimedia ad push that included the best of the traditional ad formats and the collection of new technologies available to advertisers.

CABLE AND BEYOND

When ad executives wax nostalgic about the old days, chances are good they're talking about the days before cable television. Cable took the cozy, comfortable palate of television, dominated by the Big Three networks, and blasted it into a 500+ channel media party that only continues to proliferate. The explosion presented a host of new challenges—and new opportunities—for the ad industry.

The seismic shift cable unleashed throughout the media world is well documented:

"Cable's organizational development, economic relationships, and regulatory status profoundly altered the video landscape in ways entirely unforeseen, and in the course of its growth and development many accepted notions about First Amendment rights of speakers and listeners or viewers, and about the functions and obligations of communication industries have been challenged. The cable television industry eclipsed broadcasting's asset and revenue values by the late 1980s as it created moguls and empires that joined the largest media firms in the United States. The first of many communication systems to stretch the meanings and boundaries established in the Communication Act of 1934, cable television has had a pivotal role in altering conceptions about television."[17]

Its impact on the ad industry specifically was no less dramatic. Cable's most enduring result was its offering of the alternative to broadcast—what the industry would come to call "narrowcast." This was content sliced, segmented, and targeted to a particular viewer. It started with demographics: channels for women, children, and ethnic groups. It then splintered by interest: news, weather, sports, music. Today, the focus grows even sharper with new channels tailored to Yankees fans and other tightly-knit interest groups.

Cable's ad revenues gathered slowly. Low dollar figures matched the small U.S. subscriber base. But today, three-quarters of American homes subscribe to cable, featuring all manners of content. By 1980, channels such as CNN, MTV, and ESPN were available to cable audiences, and eager consumers were tuning in. A *TV Guide* poll found that about half of TV viewers were unhappy with what they were getting on the Big Three and were eager to find new entertainment.[18]

As part of the effort to deter channel surfing, ad agencies sought to bring new levels of entertainment sophistication to TV spots. The 1984 Super Bowl featured a 60-second spot for Apple computers. The Orwellian-themed "1984" cost $500,000 to air and almost that much in production, ushering in the era of entertainment-quality Super Bowl ads.[19] Two years later, claymation technology brought ad life to the California Raisins, and by the end of the decade, Pepsi had cast Madonna and Michael Jackson in its ads. The entertainment bar had been raised. Consumers, used to a wide selection of great entertainment, demanded it whenever they looked at the screen.

The impact of cable was felt in other media. Its racier sensibilities—everything from suggestive humor to actual pornography—helped fuel the more frank use of sex in other advertising. Take for instance, a magazine ad used by Paco Rabanne to sell its cologne in the early '80s. The vignette in the ad clearly described the morning after a sexual encounter. In a phone conversation, a woman describes how her lover looked to her like a toppled Greek statue. He in return tells her how much he misses her. She then confesses to have stolen his Paco Rabanne cologne—and states her intention to rub it on her body that night to think of him.

Today, cable faces its own challenges: consolidation and turmoil in ownership, competition from other entertainment sources, and, perhaps most ironically, the challenge of yet the latest technological advances. Perhaps its greatest legacy will be that it trained the entertainment consumer to expect variety, creativity, and constant innovation. In the fragmented world created by this medium, all voices from content and ads must joust constantly for the eye of the consumer. Ending this era, the consumer eye was further enticed by a newer technology: the Internet.

Facing the era of yet another new technology, ad executives might do well to look back, not with nostalgia but with a critical eye. A new technology, a challenge to the standard modes of operation and measurement, a shake-up of the rules and expectations—advertising has been here before. While the technologies may change, the message endures. Advertising finds its way to the consumer. Ad players make sure of it.

Three

Where We Are Today

We live in an age that is constantly changing, thanks to the constant flow of information. No sooner has any one idea, business, or strategy taken hold when a dozen competitors are ready at the gate and many more are on the drawing boards. What is true, accurate, and accepted is a state that shifts every day. The digital transformation is at the root of this new reality. Every day, thanks to digital transformation, we create and store more information that for most of our history has been stored on paper. That treasure trove of knowledge, and its ability to spread globally at once-unthinkable speed, has created a world that is tough to pin down. Just when you think you know the state of something—anything—that state is already in flux, perhaps even changed completely.

Given that reality, what is the state of advertising today? It is certainly not a fixed entity. Like everything else, it is affected, influenced, and even battered by the rate and volume of digital change. The state is one of an industry at a crossroads.

We are in the midst of a media environment undergoing massive change. It is a rate of change that now occurs daily and is only accelerating. As an industry, we are often in the position of playing catch-up in this fast-changing world. Still, it's important, even crucial, to understand the realities of what we face today. Even in a changing world, they can be captured, studied, and mined for clues as to how we as an industry will need to proceed.

The hallmark of the past decade in our industry has been the advent of Internet advertising. You can see it in the numbers. The majority of 19 media measured by TNS Media Intelligence (TNS-MI) experienced growth during 2005. Internet display advertising registered the largest gain, up 13.3% to $8.3 billion on the strength of accelerated spending from dot-com brands. For the year, these online brands accounted for 49.7% of total Internet expenditures, the highest level since the dot-com bust. While some executives continued to voice concerns, budgets clearly began moving from traditional to new media. Network and spot television lost ground. Newspapers and magazines eked out single-digit gains. Meanwhile, more money than ever poured into platforms that didn't even exist a decade ago.

The Internet ad platform is a fast-moving animal, already the proud producer of a boom, bust, and renaissance in just its first few years of existence. That's more than any previous ad distribution platform can claim. And its penchant for rapid change shows no signs of slowing. We can predict and, indeed, expect that the advertising industry we experience today will be radically altered within the next several years. We are living in the digital age, on Internet time. Once you hit send, your thought is already old news. That's the theme of our industry. Everything we do will be shifted, sorted, and reconfigured by virtual technology. This is reality in the era of the one and the zero.

We are headed toward what I call Googleworld. Not so much because I think Google will emerge as a world leader—although it might—but because I know that something like it will. It's critical to understand where we are right now because our current status is what points to our certain future. Look at what we have right now:

Fragmented Media: This commonly used term actually has three distinct parts. As Jupiter Research analyst David Schatsky points out in his January 2006 blog entry, fragmentation has three current dimensions.[1] On its most basic level, it is the breakup of the mass audience. What was once the mass market is now a kaleidoscope of network, cable, satellite, radio, newspaper, magazine, Web site, blog, DVR, MP3, and many, many more. Media, already split into a million little pieces, are only poised for more. The trend toward narrowcasting is accelerating.

In its second dimension, fragmentation describes the way consumers personally experience the splinter effect. Now, with more choices, the entertainment and information focus of individual consumers' attention spans is spread across all the forms of traditional media and now the additional forms of new media—Internet, video games, podcasts, and others.

Eager to stay in front of distractible consumers, media companies have been willing to split, slice, and dice themselves and their content into smaller portion sizes. Fragmentation is not a one-time event but a constant in the life of the industry today.

Convergence: The melding of devices, promised in the early '90s, is here. And smart advertisers are all over the trend. Daily, the industry serves up another major marketer stepping into the digital dreamworks and embracing the change as a point of leverage. Take, for example, the efforts of Toyota and the marketing of its vehicle Yaris.

In the spring of 2006, one of the hottest shows on television was FOX Network's *Prison Break*. The action-packed drama followed the exploits of a young attractive hero who got himself incarcerated with the express purpose of staging an escape for himself and his wrongly convicted brother, an inmate at the same maximum-security facility. Each week brought new tales of the hero's daring exploits behind the prison walls, his friends on the outside, and the conspiratorial forces that gathered against him. The fan base grew. The buzz was positive. The show drew raves from critics for its fast pace and gripping story line.

But *Prison Break* wasn't just hot thanks to its content. It had another reason to draw accolades. It was the platform for a brave new format of advertising. About halfway through the season, car maker Toyota signed on as a sponsor. In a deal worth an industry-estimated $10 million, Toyota agreed to buy traditional commercial time, space in a dedicated Web site, product placement in the show itself, and, in a leap forward for the advertising industry, 26 "mobisodes" designed to be viewed and enjoyed on the screen of a cell phone.

These mobisodes—a term FOX trademarked to describe the new format—were original content, developed to run as a complimentary story line to the prime TV programming. They followed the arc of a new character and her parallel plotline to the prime-time TV action. And each episode was prefaced by a specially designed 10-second ad spot featuring Toyota's new vehicle, Yaris.

"We're utilizing this emerging entertainment medium as a way to provide fans of *Prison Break* with details about the show courtesy of Yaris," said Jim Farley, vice president of marketing for Toyota at the time of the deal in Spring 2006. "Our partnership with FOX provides an exclusive portal to showcase Yaris to consumers in a fun way where they can discover more about the car on their own time."[2]

Consumer Choice: The rise of the Internet means consumers have the ability to say no to anything that doesn't quite meet their standards. Don't like a local retailer? Shop online. Displeased with what your local movie theater is showing? Download something more entertaining. Bored by an ad? Skip it. Consumers have been digitally transformed into active, vocal markets that companies are wholly unused to serving. But some smart marketers are leaning to embrace, rather than fear, this awakened giant. After fretting over how consumers may skip, block, or avoid their ads altogether, advertisers are embracing the reality of consumer control and are leveraging it for ad purposes.

Take, for example, the recent effort by Burger King. The perennial number-two burger chain made a strong push in its marketing to connect with young men—a demographic that likes to hang out on the Internet. In an accident of extra merchandise, it discovered a way to embrace consumer control and turn it into a marketing coup. The site owners of Heavy.com, a site that sponsors and promotes user-generated content, convinced Burger King executives to part with a few dozen king masks—copies of the ones used in the TV commercials. At first, the fast food giant was leery—give the customer control of the company icon? But execs were convinced to take the risk.

Consumers rewarded them. Mask recipients stepped up by the dozens and began creating their own ads using the king mask. Heavy.com posted almost all of them—editing a few for overly raunchy content. The site tracked more than nine million visitors to the Burger King videos, and the burger chain racked up dozens of press notices for its creative foray into the brave new world of advertising to empowered consumers. It was an example of more than just clever advertising. It was evidence that the industry is overcoming its fear of the digital marketplace.

Even media themselves are showing a willingness to step off the sidelines. Magazines, long resisters of the Internet trend, are stepping into the spotlight. In the spring of 2006, Condé Nast Publications prepared to launch a site for its highly coveted teen girl readers with content not by its staff of fashion editors but instead by the readers themselves. A site devoted to user-generated content is not utterly unheard of, but one created by a major old-line magazine company breaks the mold.

Speed of Delivery: There was a day when marketers like FedEx could make a big point of showing off their ability to deliver an item overnight. At the time, that seemed quite speedy. Today, of course, overnight is practically overdue. Years ago, when working on my doctoral dissertation, I spent three months tracking down an obscure manuscript. At the time, I was quite pleased with my efforts. Today, I would have been impatient if the search had taken me more than an hour on the Internet. And the generation growing up with the Internet is even more time pressed. They bail if a Web page takes any time at all to load. Life is too short to suffer slow-moving bandwidth. We live in an era where speed of delivery is here and getting faster.

Networks are beginning to recognize this need for speed. Among their latest offerings: downloads of just-aired TV episodes. The product recognizes a key shift in the consumer time frame. No longer will consumers wait patiently for a DVD release or a spate of summer reruns to enjoy a first-run episode. The gratification must be quicker. And networks, long used to setting the schedules to suit their own purposes, are more and more starting to make the shift to consumer time.

Technology miniaturization: The old saw—location, location, location—is dead. It really doesn't matter where you are. The amazing shrinking screen now means you can get your information, your entertainment, and your advertising anywhere you want to be: in your home, in the office, on the road, on the beach. Miniaturization makes it as easy as carrying a wallet. And that only improves with technology. Can Dick Tracy's watch be far off? It may already be for sale on the Internet.

24/7 access: We live in a world that is always on, which means that as an industry we must do more than fill 30-second spots and gatefold spreads. In a world where media are on all the time, we as an industry find ourselves asked to manage that vastly expanded universe.

WHERE DOES THAT LEAVE US?

How can all this upheaval give us any clues? It helps, I think, to look at the state of change from the consumer perspective. For everything that we have experienced as an industry, look, for a moment, at the state of today's consumers:

- More information is available than ever before.
- More information sources are available than ever before.
- Information comes at them faster than ever before.
- Content can find them anywhere they go.
- They want information fast.
- They want it to be accurate.

- They want it to be entertaining.
- There are still only 24 hours in the day.

A Day in the Life of a Consumer: 2007

At the dawn of the digital era, the most desirable target customers are those who have both the interest in the new technology and the means to purchase it. Researchers at IBM coined a phrase to describe these individuals: gadgetiers.[3] These consumers are the first of the "lean-forward" generation. While the other adults of their era may still be content to lean back and enjoy media served up mass-market style, this cutting-edge group embraces new technology and new media choices. And while younger consumers may also share a passion for new technology, the gadgetier generation has an edge. They are consumers in the prime of their earning power. Marketers are eager to reach them and to tap their ready spending.

These consumers are of two minds when it comes to ads. Some they welcome because it informs and educates them about new products and services, but others they find intrusive and unwanted, and they look for technological ways to block them from interfering with their day.

The lean-forward day starts early. Consumers hook up to MP3 devices—more than 18 million devices are in use.[4] Jupiter Research estimates that 90% of U.S. consumers have 1,000 or fewer songs in their digital music collections, and 60% have fewer than 200.[5] Consumers listen via ear buds on the train or piped through car stereos. Satellite radio remains an interesting offering, but so far, it is not a major factor in the day of these consumers' lives.

Almost at work, consumers may make a last check of their PDAs—a scan for messages and news alerts to which they subscribe, including sports scores, market news, and weather. More than 15 million devices are in use. Upon arrival at the office, attention shifts from a portable small screen to a desktop. Consumers dart all day between the corporate Intranet and work-related Web sites. They read a number of publications, including daily newspapers and monthly trade magazines, online. Consumers also receive daily updates from most-favored publications via e-mail.

The workday is centered around technology tools. Google and Yahoo! serve as information sources. The company e-mail connects the consumers not only to the outside world but also to offices just steps away. E-mail is a source of information: professional, personal, and commercial. Consumers use it to stay abreast of all of these topics throughout the day.

At the day's end, consumers take their mobile phones in hand for the trip home. While ownership of mobile phones is high, subscription to services such as videos and games remains low. This class of consumers is most concerned about the price and reliability of phone service.

Once at home, the consumers' focus on media and technology shifts from work and convenience to family and entertainment. They use the family DVR to collect relevant entertainment content. Consumers subscribe to pay services that allow them access to coverage of favorite sports teams—even those in remote cities. Although they have the ability to skip ads, they still watch many, especially those that are funny or from industries in which the consumers are eager to learn of new products and services. Tapping the increasing popularity of home Wi-Fi systems, consumers bring laptops to the living room and multitask while watching television. Consumers may surf the Internet, answer personal e-mails, or handle a work-related chore.

Come late night, the gadget-oriented consumers may shift to the home PC. They may preview tomorrow's headlines or check late sports scores. Many read and post to blogs and online forums that pertain to hobbies and nonwork interests. They end by checking the weather for tomorrow's commute and power down for the night.

Rapid and profound change, in the industry and in the lives of consumers, has put advertising at a crossroads. But it's consumers who are going to lead us along the right path. Consumers still want advertising—but in a way that functions in the digitally transformed, 24/7, miniaturized, faster-than-a-speeding-bullet environment. Consumers, at the crossroads, want a sign. In the digital age, those signs will be provided by search technology.

Indeed, those who are most adept at providing search signage for consumers will take leadership roles in the digital age. Search will become the critical tool for consumers looking to navigate the brave new world. It is the organizer that will make the digitally transformed marketplace function for both consumers and advertisers. Leveraging this technology will lead us from the state of flux we are now in to the marketing nirvana we all desire: one-to-one communication.

We are at a crossroads, but consumers have pointed the way for us. The road ahead will be paved by search. Instead of theory, we'll rely on intentions to direct our messaging. Interests indicated through search behavior point the way to one-to-one marketing. Advanced search algorithms provide the vehicle that will connect consumers with marketers in the brave new world.

Still, it takes courage and initiative to choose the path ahead, and the advertising industry today is not fully engaged in its journey. In his address to the 2006 American Association of Advertising Agencies (AAAA) Management Conference for Agency CEOs, Anthony J. Hopp, association chairman and CEO of agency Campbell-Ewald, chided his fellow executives for their industry-wide funk. In other industry meetings, he said, the news is good: innovation is on the rise, new technologies are emerging, competition is thriving.

Not so, he said, at our industry gatherings.

"What comes out of our advertising conferences? Here's a sampling from the last five or six years:

- The death of the 30-second spot
- The threat of the Internet
- Clients not valuing all that we do
- Insufficient compensation
- Consumers stealing control from us."[6]

Hopp compared ad industry executives to the anxiety-prone Charlie Brown of "Peanuts" comic strip fame—a character who could look at something wonderful, like Christmas, and still find a problem. "Can't we sense the potential?" Hopp asked the crowd.

At this point in the industry's history, some can. Many challenges face this industry—challenges brought about by new technology, demanding consumers, and a fragmenting audience. But after years of testing, hesitating, and worrying over these changes, marketers are taking the plunge. They are stepping into the fray and looking for new, creative, technologically infused ways to participate in the digital dream. What is the state of advertising today? It is an industry stepping over the starting line into its new era. It is an industry at its crossroads—taking its first steps onto the new path.

Four

The Three Futures of Advertising

Advertising is no stranger to forecasting. It's part of the industry's core competency. We are forever investigating, divining, and peering into our industrial crystal balls for the vision of what's to come. It's in large part what clients hire agencies to do—predict the future. Figuring out what's next takes up much of our present.

But these days, those skills are being called upon for more than just client work. Today, we find ourselves turning the crystal ball inward, examining the hallmarks and challenges of our own industry, and struggling to put a clear forecast on the future of our industry. It is no easy task. And it's further complicated by the proliferation of paths forward.

The experience of the thinker at the crossroads is not unique. Robert Frost depicted it eloquently in his poem "The Road Not Taken":

> "Two roads diverged in a yellow wood,
> And sorry I could not travel both
> And be one traveler, long I stood
> And looked down one as far as I could
> To where it bent in the undergrowth."[1]

The ad industry has taken that image one better. There are not just two but probably three roads ahead. Each leads the industry toward a different future, and to date, no path is holding a concrete lead. The industry will need to decide which road to follow, which future to choose.

THREE ROADS TO THE FUTURE

#1: The Conservative Path

There is a near-term future for the ad industry—one that is not at all impossible to imagine—that has almost all of us playing defense.

Advertising agencies, in an effort to protect their position as arbiters of ad spending, will look to slow the move toward new technologies and keep the industry firmly in the formats ad leaders know so well. While testing will go on in the areas of digital technology—the use of leading-edge tactics like VOD and interactive advertising—the bulk of the ad work will continue to be housed in the power troika of television, print, and radio.

In client pitches, agencies will tout the reliability and strong history of these media. Television, they will argue, is in virtually every home, the entertainment center of almost every American family. It is the entertainment format of choice for the mass market in America, and there is currently no technology that comes close to its adoption rate. Every home in America, from the poorest to the richest, sports a television. And that box is not static in its offerings. From its early handful of networks, it has grown to now showcase cable and network channels and a host of new programming. It is the screen that brings everything from the most popular mass program to the most niche cable show. There is nothing yet that challenges the supremacy of the small screen.

What's more is that in this conservative future scenario, agencies will push back the notion that traditional print—in particular the newspaper—is in peril. If television could not convince consumers to give up reading the paper, what's to suggest that any other new technology will be able to do so? Even in the Internet age, consumers say they like the feel of the paper in their hands, the weight of the book, the wide scope of the broadsheet, the glossy look of the magazine layout. No new medium has ever wiped out the one that came before it; print remains a viable advertising platform.

Agencies on this conservative path will counsel their clients to test the new technologies and make small experiments in efforts such as interactive advertising and use of new screens like the cell phone and the movie theater. Resist overspending in these newfangled formats. The mantra will be: use what works. Putting the relationship with the consumer at risk by advertising in these unproven formats is unwise, they'll argue. The full force and talent of the ad world is experienced in the art of the existing ad: the 30-second spot, the radio jingle, the classified, the four-color spread. These are the formats that brought big brands into an era of unprecedented success both in the United States and globally. Ditching them now would be too risky. Better to take it slow and see how these new formats develop while keeping the bulk of the ad budget in areas we know can work.

Conservative marketers will embrace that advice with relief and resolve. Corporate leaders who find themselves in an era packed with near-term goals and a demand for immediate ROI will initially rejoice to find out their tried-and-true tactics are still in the arsenal. Today's marketing chiefs have precious little time to prove to higher-ups that their strategies are working. Putting finite resources into tactics that have yet no accurate measurement strikes many as insanely dangerous. Sticking the money into a tactic that has decades of measurement history behind it is, at least initially, reassuring.

Marketers will come to meetings, able to follow the conversation, experienced enough in the traditional tactics to participate, and able to take the plan up the food chain with the confidence that comes from tactical experience. Doing what worked last year—and the year before and the year before—will be far more appealing than the call to dive into something experimental and new. Brand building will be mapped out as it has been for a generation, by using mass-market techniques, putting the lion's share of marketing resources into television and print, and tapping long-established measurement systems to determine how well these ads are working.

Media will perhaps be the most eager to travel the conservative route because they have the most to lose if another path is chosen. The conservative path—one that focuses on traditional ad formats and keeps to long-standing measurement codes—is the financial backbone of modern media. The accepted relationship, in which marketers buy time and space from media outlets as their entrée into the lives of consumers, is one that funds the world of television, newspapers, and magazines. The idea that a marketer could tap a new medium—one not in the current club—or even more scary, go around media and connect directly to consumers on digital platforms, is a nightmare scenario. Traditional media, not surprisingly, are the champions of tradition.

To this end, media will travel the conservative path and will trumpet their history, their reliability, and their longtime relationships with marketers. Media will cite the strong and resilient history of newspapers. New media have come along before, yet consumers still turn to the broadsheet for the day's news, weather, sports, and entertainment information. It remains the platform of the employer seeking workers, the politician seeking votes, and the retailer seeking foot traffic. No medium has yet unseated it, and it remains a vital core of the information flow.

Likewise, media will demonstrate the staying power of television. Like the newspaper, television has read its own obit many times. First, it was predicted, cable would kill the network. Didn't happen. Then, the pundits proclaimed, the remote would undermine the medium. Yet it remains. And further attacks have come, from the VCR, the DVR, the Internet, the DVD. And still, television remains the single biggest media platform in world history, yet unrivaled, yet untoppled by would-be successors. Whoever says the 30-second spot is dead hasn't paid attention while dozens of marketers shell out millions to be seen during the commercial breaks of the Super Bowl, the Academy Awards, or critical episodes of prime-time television. Appointment television holds audience, they'll argue. It's up to the industry to protect it from erosion.

Indeed, much of the energy spent on the conservative path will be in the act of protection. Agencies, marketers, and media will look for rules and regulations that hold back invaders of their business space. Technologies that block or avoid ads will be decried. Systems that circumvent or displace marketing messages will be kept out of consumers' hands. The conservative future is one of protectionist policies and good defense, a fortified castle that keeps safe the historical ruler of the media landscape.

But the fortress has cracks. The choice of a conservative future may hold off change for some time—maybe even a long time—but not permanently. And in the intervening years, when the ad world avoids internal change, it will be happening outside the walls, unchecked.

It's instructive to look at what happened to the computer industry in the 1980s. The ruling class of that industry was well established in the business of mainframes—a business that looked to other businesses as customers. The industry rejected the early notion of the personal computer and did not embrace the concept that individual consumers could have a role in their technical choices. To hold off the change, the industry took a defensive mode. Hardware and software were designed for use by technical professionals. The sales process was strictly controlled as a business-to-business experience. The industry presented itself as the holder of critical expertise, one that could not be replaced.

But while the computer industry built its business fortress, change simply moved to another spot on the game board and forged ahead. While big companies held the line on their traditional sales and marketing plans, smaller upstarts made their way into the industry.

These companies that would one day be household names—Dell, Gateway, and others—began making cheaper, easier, more accessible personal computers and began marketing them to consumers. The question of whether personal computers would replace mainframes was taken out of the small circle of technical experts and thrown wide to the mass market for review. The start-ups were small at first, but their popularity grew, and these businesses began to nibble at the giants. Eventually, they were able to work into the industry from the bottom up and forced the mainframe makers into a price war and ultimately undermined the supremacy of the supercomputer in the technical world.

As the attack from the bottom progressed, many leading players, such as IBM, were caught looking like dinosaurs in a changing world. In the end, they had to abandon their defense mindset and compete with these start-ups on the newly created personal computer playing field.

Advertising is likely to face a similar fate. It may travel the conservative road. It may hold off change for some period of time. But that will only give upstarts a chance to attack from the bottom. And when that happens, the traditional ad world will, eventually, be forced to compete in that new world and on the competition's terms. Agencies, marketers, and media may take what they view as a "safe" road, but it's only the long road to change. Just as the computing world discovered, change does not cease because you refuse to embrace it. It only finds another way to undermine your best-laid plans.

#2: The Path of Change

This is the path on which the future is one of reconciliation. This is the path on which we all concede that the change that buffets our industry today is not temporal. It is not a wrinkle, a hurdle, or a short-term challenge. It is a permanent change. Accepting that reality puts us on this path that embraces change yet respects the dislocation and uncertainty it produces. It is a path of change, with compromise—a path that acknowledges the future without dropkicking the past to the curb.

On this path, the dual realities—call them analog and digital—will exist side by side. The industry will tap them both to maintain connection to the consumer in the present day while preparing for the gradual but inevitable move to the newer platform.

For agencies, this path will mean a shift in the arsenal. Instead of a full range of traditional tactics and a few side experiments, the palate available will need to be split more evenly—even 50-50—between traditional and new media options. While classic tactics such as newspaper and TV advertising will remain in the mix, they will need to share the stage with the growing roster of new media options such as Video on Demand (VOD), cell phone and Personal Digital Assistant (PDA) advertising, search, and interactive creations yet untested. The two classes of creativity will need to exist side by side in the agency roster and carry equal weight in the strategies.

Some agencies are already primed for this arrangement. For others, it will require change: perhaps new talent, a new organizational structure, and a new paradigm for dealing with clients and critics. Indeed, the most dramatic shift for agencies may be cultural rather than tactical. Talented professionals can always learn to use new tools. But it's these same professionals that will have to step out on to the path of change before that learning can take place.

The path of change will also be a challenge to marketers. Marketers, protective of their scarce marketing resources, will hardly find good news in the concept that this money will have to be divided among old and new tactics. But recognition that change can't be held off indefinitely will make the coexistence option more attractive. It won't mean abandoning old tactics, just mixing them with the new. For many companies, this will mean that brand campaigns and other efforts will become more complex and multi-pronged efforts. While a brand might once have debuted supported by television and print, in this version of the future, that brand will need a full orchestra of media behind it—the traditional television and print and an equal helping of new technologies. They might be video or music downloadable to a cell phone, a virtual campaign backed by blog and e-mail efforts, or a high-concept ad designed to be shown on a movie theater screen.

Forward-thinking marketers will also see this as an opportunity—a chance to reach out across the divide and make connections with the up-and-coming generation of consumers. The next wave will be one that embraces technology as a natural part of everyday life. Smart marketers will see the side-by-side arrangement of using new and old technologies as a way to learn the new language and make initial connections with this new breed of consumers. Few companies will be bold enough to ditch their old strategies. They'll worry about losing their base market share—those weaned on the familiar ad formats of 30-second spots and radio jingles. But they'll recognize the need to service both the old and the new consumers, and this path of change will give them a viable method to make that happen.

Media will need to adapt their product offerings to be ready to serve this split-screen strategy. To keep agencies and marketers happy, media will need both traditional and new distribution options. So the traditional broadsheet will still roll off the presses, but it will be complemented by a digital option—perhaps an online version of the newspaper, or e-mail delivery, or a version downloadable to the latest PDA. And just as the content will live in two worlds, so too must the advertising options. Media will need to make the case for both traditional and digital platforms and offer them side by side to marketers on the path of change.

All media will develop these digital options—old and new versions to operate in concert. Magazines will produce print and online content. Broadcast will embrace appointment television and the DVR. Music will arrive via airwaves and via download. Advertising options will be constructed so that buyers can choose—one, the other, or both—to make their connection to consumers.

This path to change is actually an interim step. It's a stepping stone to the broader experience of convergence. But for many in the industry, it may be the necessary first step.

#3: Digital Dreaming

The third possible future for our industry is one in which we leave behind old rules and realities and step fully into the technological possibilities. It is a future in which we don't look back. It is the bravest of all possible options, and it's open to us—should we actually manage to lose our fear of change.

In the digital dreaming future, content is defined not by its old media name but by its core property: text, video, and audio. All content, clarified and freed, can be distributed via any converged technology. Consumers will control this content. They will decide what they see, how they see it, when they see it, and where they see it. Households will have a hardware distribution service that will deliver this content on the consumers' demand, on the consumers' terms.

In the digital dream, all information in the world is ultimately accessible. The question becomes, how do we look at all this information in a coherent and useful way? The answer already exists. It is search. Search algorithms become the method by which we extract the vast world of digital information and make it work for us. Search becomes the organizer, the card catalogue, the method by which information is sliced, diced, and reconfigured to be useful rather than overwhelming.

Search does not solve the industry's problems. It does not fix bad advertising or compensate for lazy, uncreative messaging. Instead, it drives messaging forward by tapping into the most powerful of consumer emotions: intentions. Search reveals the one thing marketers yearn to know: what do customers want? Search reveals an intentions history, it unveils the interests that can lead to one-to-one marketing, and it provides a technologically advanced way to understand consumer desire.

This setup turns traditional advertising on its head. In the digital dreaming future, the measurement of the mass market becomes obsolete. Instead of crafting a construct in which we hope to make connections with consumers, we are able to do it in a targeted and efficient way by tailoring ads to consumer behavior. With their behavior, consumers tell us what they want, and the ad industry responds in kind. ROI becomes a reality. Consumers are empowered to say exactly what they want. Advertising efficiencies, freed from the mass-market approach, soar.

The implications for the digital dreaming future are enormous. In this future, advertising becomes independent of content. It finds its consumers not through information or entertainment services but by tapping demographics and behavioral signals.

How will this work? Consumers will be offered a choice: pay a fee for ad-free access to content or opt for free access with targeted advertising. Contrary to the fears of many marketers, most consumers will not choose to live in the ad-free world. Most appreciate that advertising plays a role in their decision making. Consumers want to learn about new brands, they want to know about the changes and possibilities of existing brands, and they certainly want to know the latest in pricing.

But this advertising will not look like the old advertising. It will all be interactive and delivered on digital platforms. Media mix modeling will no longer be relevant because the placement of these ads will not be based on who watches or listens to what. Instead, all advertising will be available to consumers when they are logged on to their converged device, no matter what they are using the device for—entertainment, news, business, or pleasure. The ads will be delivered based on demographics and behavior. The consumers receive them at will.

What's the economic engine of this consumer nirvana? One possible model is this: The advertiser creates an ad program and wants to get it in front of interested consumers. That company in today's world would go to a media firm—a CBS or an ESPN—and buy time to show the ad, in hopes that the audience demographics would result in a sale. In the new age, the advertiser will approach the new gatekeeper—a search firm. These new gatekeepers won't own content. Instead, they will own the environment in which the consumers seek it. They will be the organizational system consumers rely on to sort and deliver content to any number of technological devices.

Advertisers will pay the gatekeeper, which has the technology, research, and delivery systems to get that ad to the target consumers.

Content providers will also approach the gatekeeper, eager to reach consumers with their product. And here's where the money is made: when a consumer is enjoying content, the gatekeeper will serve up advertising based on the history of intentions it has built up on that customer. If the consumer clicks on the ad, the advertiser has secured an interested customer, and the gatekeeper pays the content provider a royalty fee.

The specifics of pricing and other details would need to be worked out. But the scenario has many winners: the gatekeeper can't lose; it has been paid up front. The advertiser lays out cash but has a greater chance of making a connection with interested consumers, thanks to the gatekeeper's technology. The content provider is free of advertiser influence and other constraints. And, of course, consumers get ads tailored to their desires and the ability to access these ads without missing a minute of entertainment content.

Ad invitations will come on the basis of consumer behavior and will operate independently of the content themes. So consumers in the market for a new car will receive information targeted to that goal, no matter whether they're watching the evening news, downloading music, or checking sports scores.

It's not the only way to construct a working revenue model, but it's one to consider because it is rational and provides economic incentives dynamically throughout the process. There are ways in which this digital dream will generate money for its players.

Day in the Life of a Consumer: 2015

The target consumers of the near future will be young people, weaned on technology. These are the members of Generation Y, and a day in their lives in the near future will show them coming into their prime consuming years. Born in the era of cable television and the emergence of the Internet, they will have lived their entire lives with an array of choices and a constant supply of new technological opportunities. They are consumers always looking for the next best thing. They expect to find out about it via a mix of corporate messaging and peer recommendations. They don't wait for any one message to come to them; they seek out new information on a regular basis.

They live most of their media lives on multiple screens and sort content into three parts: video, text, and audio. The device on which the information arrives is irrelevant because they toggle back and forth among them all throughout the day. Video plays a key part of the entertainment world, although these consumers consider the notion of "appointment television" to be quaint at best. These consumers manage their TV viewing through home technology systems. Using DVRs, they seek out content they like and rely upon recommendations from peers as well as their search service provider to suggest new items. They make their own viewing schedule and coordinate it with friends and family. When it comes to seeking out new programs, they expect advice on two fronts: the recommendation of friends and the results of the home technology system's search algorithm. They know the technology is tailored to tweeze out preferences, and they expect it to serve up usable suggestions. They will ditch a search service that fails to meet their needs and will use more than one to be sure they are getting the full picture.

When it comes to TV advertising, these consumers opt to get free service in return for their eyeballs on the commercial breaks. They are aware that they have the option to pay for ad-free television, but the price is high by their standards and not worth the effort. Besides, they figure, ads are a good way to learn about what's out in the marketplace and where the best deals may be.

While they consent to the advertising, they have high standards for it. Ads that are irrelevant, dull, or incomplete in their information draw disdain, and these consumers freely share critiques with peers and corporate marketers on blogs and Web sites. A poor ad will color the overall impression of a brand. They embrace the branded entertainment trend so long as the entertainment is top quality. If it's poor, they will think less of the brand for making the deal—and more important, they will pick up the remote and click away.

On the desktop, they often seek commercial content as they shop for new products and services. They frequently visit the corporate sites of the brands and tap the sites for information, deals, and entertaining content. For those at the top of the desirability list, these consumers opt for an RSS feed to be connected to the latest news. They also read and post to blogs that cover the technology and entertainment that interests them. Their primary ad experience on the desktop comes via search. Using sites that track their behavior, they know to look at the side columns for links that may take them to products and services they seek. They consider banner ads and other billboards to be untargeted and rarely tailored to their needs. The computer is the first place they turn when ready to shop for a new product or service, and they view it as a key conduit of commercial information. Often, as they close in on a purchase decision, they will use the desktop to ask direct questions of company representatives or other company customers. They may tap live chat or e-mail to make this connection.

Finally, the small screen plays a primary role in their lives as consumers. They look at it constantly when away from home as they check for messages, news, and other real-time information. They use search on their cells to find stores, restaurants, and other destinations. They rely on this third screen to be "always on" so that they can send and receive information. They often download entertainment to their cells for enjoyment away from home. It can take the form of music, games, or specially designed episodes of a favorite TV show or movie. They also access branded entertainment via the cell phone, fully aware of the marriage between content and corporate sponsor.

These consumers' media and willingness to receive information are always on. They do not consider commercial time to be separate from entertainment time, and they expect all of the media to be fast, accessible, visually gripping, and relevant to their circumstances.

Still, many truisms are erased in the era of digital dreaming. Rules of creative development, distribution, audience measurement, and effectiveness are rewritten. But this is not an impossible dream. Indeed, it is a viable path for the industry to choose. It is also the one calling for the most courage.

Five

The Empowered Consumer

"It's not just selection, but information. I'm shopping for a small form factor computer right now. Back in the day I would have had to just walk into Best Buy and get whatever they have, but now I've read detailed—and I mean detailed—reviews on all the top models, with fine-grained comparisons and recommendations. I don't buy anything any more without researching all the alternatives. I don't know how people spent money before the internet."[1]

—ANONYMOUS SHOPPER, WWW.WASHINGTONMONTHLY.COM

It may be a challenging time to be in advertising, but it's a great time to be a consumer. Today's consumers face none of the constraints present just a few short years ago. Many of the day-to-day annoyances of the consumer experience have been virtually eliminated by changes and expansions in technology. Consumers were once dependent upon a whole array of professionals in retailing and advertising for news of and access to products and services. But today, that dependent relationship has been substantially reconfigured. Today's consumers put up with few of yesterday's regular obstacles. Consider:

- Can't make time to get to the store? The Internet is open 24/7.
- Missed a first-run movie with your favorite actor? The DVD is on its way.

- Waiting for the perfect time to buy a new product? An e-mail newsletter will keep you updated on price changes.
- Miss your hometown newspaper? Read the digital version online.
- Favorite TV show in conflict with your poker game? A DVR solves that problem.
- Bored or annoyed by a TV ad? Pick up the remote and zap it.
- Shopping for a big-ticket item? Research it online, sans pushy salesperson.
- Want to know everything there is to know about a new product? Don't stop at the advertising. Tap into blogs and other consumer-generated content for the straight scoop.

Consumers have power as never before, and they are wielding it like thunderbolts in the marketplace. They are bypassing advertising by using search to generate their own product research and upending the rules of marketing today by accessing news and entertainment when they want, where they want, and under the circumstances of their choosing. The notion of the family gathered around the living room television during prime time, dutifully accepting the prearranged marketing message, is now a quaint image of time gone by. Consumers today are leaned forward, technology in hand, masters of the buying and selling experience. The era of empowered consumers is here.

The initial response from media and advertisers has been less than enthusiastic. Indeed, the new breed of customers, technology in hand, is considered armed and dangerous. Empowered consumers create all kinds of havoc in a carefully constructed economic model. Long-held concepts such as day parts, ratings, and paid circulation lose their meaning in the world where consumers are in control. Consider the comments of iMedia Columnist Steve Rubel at the iMedia Brand Summit in March 2005. He was responding to statements by

Jack Trout, the legendary ad/marketing consultant and author of numerous books on the industry:

> "This is not a threat but an opportunity. And unfortunately not everybody recognizes this. Take a load of this quote: 'It's a real problem …'—we're talking about amateur ads—'… and the problem gets bigger the more people see this stuff. It begins to muddy the message. The ad industry should rise up against these amateurs.' Well, Jack Trout said that. I mean, Jack, I love your books, but I think that's crazy."[2]

That craziness had its share of followers. Early attempts to deal with empowered consumers have centered on taking back some of that power. Technology companies have lobbied for devices that prevent ad skipping. Owners of entertainment content have looked for ways to keep their wares off the virtual market. Lawsuits have been filed to stop bloggers from spreading their own form of brand-related messaging. Rules, devices, and lawsuits have been leveraged in an attempt to regain control of the relationship. The advertising industry and all its players have tried hard to push back.

While some of this may work in the short run, ultimately, it's an exercise in futility. The industry may pine for the old days in which consumers were passive, activated on cue by ads and services sent out into the marketplace. But wishing will not make it so, and blocking consumers from exercising power will only promote backlash. Consumers have little loyalty to their advertising providers. If one company attempts to stymie their power, consumers will simply switch to another that allows them free reign. And there are many competitors willing to offer that freedom. Having tasted empowerment, it's unlikely that consumers will agree to go back to the state of childlike dependency. Instead, the industry will need to step up and deal with this new breed of customers on its own terms.

How can the industry cope with the new and empowered consumers? First, a definition of terms.

WHAT ARE EMPOWERED CONSUMERS?

Active

Sit today's consumers on the sofa next to those from the era gone by and you can immediately see the difference. The old consumers lean back, get comfortable, and wait for news, entertainment, and advertising to wash over them. They're used to receiving data this way—in a state of recline. While they may make some initial choices about the channel to watch, the content to enjoy, and the time of their date with appointment television, they leave much of the decision making up to the faceless executives behind the media companies. Their role: recipients.

Beside them are today's empowered consumers. And in every way that the old consumers are passive, these new ones are active. Instead of leaning back, these consumers lean forward. Their TV viewing is punctuated by active choices. They review the channels for programming options. They may use a VCR or DVR to choose from programming that isn't being broadcast at the moment they sit down. They'll tap these devices further to fast-forward or skip through advertising. Even without the latest technology, they're unwilling to be as passive as their neighbors. They use their remote control to channel surf, adjust the sound and visual experience, and joyride through other channels during commercial breaks.

To empowered consumers, media are a participation sport. They enter the arena, searching for what they want, adept at getting it and getting it on their own terms. The lean-back passivity of just a few years ago strikes them now as a waste of time. Just as they actively manage their work and hobbies, they bring that initiative to their media. Their role: directors.

Tech-Savvy

It's technology that puts the power in the hands of consumers. Remotes allow consumers to channel surf. DVRs and VCRs exacerbate this process. The Internet allows consumers to shop unfettered by time or space. Miniaturization allows consumers to take their media any place they want, in a device that fits in their coat pockets. And the tech options just keep on coming. Just as media adjust to one new set of machine-enhanced behaviors, new options are for sale.

In addition to using technology to receive media, consumers use technology to customize the media experience. Users can decide when media are on, when content arrives, and in what format. What's more is that savvy tech users can craft a personalized media experience by cherry-picking music for an individualized listening experience or arranging content for their own versions of must-see TV.

Demanding

Empowered consumers want it now. Right now—if not sooner. The advent of fast and effective technology has produced a distinct behavior modification in today's consumers. Speed is not a desire; it's a requirement. And the definition of speedy service becomes more stringent by the day. There was a time when finding information on the Internet was such a revelation; we basked in its marvel. Just a couple keystrokes and the world was before you on the screen. But a few short years later, it's as though the consumer attention span has been shrunk to seconds. Now, if a page takes even 10 seconds to load, our fingers twitch impatiently over the keyboard, and our attention is poised to bolt. Technology-enhanced media are so fast, so appealing, so good at making consumers happy, that we have learned to take it as a given and demand more. More, better, faster. Empowered consumers have made demands and seen them met. They will only make more and expect that these too will be speedily addressed.

On 24/7

Once upon a time, there was a schedule for good times and bad times to try to reach consumers. But that timed concept has been erased—

along with long-held assumptions about day parts, prime time, and business hours. Today's empowered consumers are on whenever they want to be, and that can be for one hour a day or 24/7. They make that call. So the advertiser that wants to reach consumers must cope with empowered consumers who are utterly without loyalty to time.

The lean-back, passive consumers were trained to read a newspaper in the morning, do business during 9 to 5, and sit back and watch appointment television in the evening.

Today's empowered consumers may engage a series of RSS downloads in the morning, listen to satellite radio on the way to work, combine business tasks with personal chores such as shopping while using the company computer, and select from a prerecorded menu of entertainment options at night. Or they might reverse these activities and catch the latest crime drama in the early morning hours, tap into the news during their lunch hour, and shop during what used to be considered prime time for TV advertisers.

The concept of time has been completely co-opted by empowered consumers. It all happens now on their watch. Physicist Alan Lightman in his novel *Einstein's Dreams* describes the way the world would work absent the tyranny of linear time:

> "In a world where time cannot be measured, there are no clocks, no calendars, no definite appointments. Events are triggered by other events, not by time. A house is begun when stone and lumber arrive at the building site. The stone quarry delivers stone when the quarryman needs money. The barrister leaves home to argue a case at the Supreme Court when his daughter makes a joke about his growing bald. Education at the gymnasium in Berne is concluded when the student has passed his examinations. Trains leave the station at Bahnhofplatz when the cars are filled with passengers."[3]

In many ways, empowered consumers create this time-free experience by refusing to follow the old business-hour rules. As the old ballad from the band Chicago goes: *Does anybody really know what time it is? Does anybody really care?* Today's answer: No. Today's empowered consumers do not care what time it is. It is always consumer time.

Overwhelmed

Still, it is not all nirvana in the world of empowered consumers. While much of the newness drives directly to their benefit, plenty of what has washed into the consumer space over the past decade has created its own set of problems. Consider the comments of psychology professor Barry Schwartz in his book *The Paradox of Choice*:

> "As the number of choices grows further the negatives escalate until we become overloaded. At this point, choice no longer liberates, but debilitates. It might even be said to tyrannize."[4]

Today's consumers have unlimited choices. Like the experience of the kid in the candy store, that can seem great at first, overwhelming a bit later, and finally, the producer of a serious stomachache. When consumers get everything, they find that managing everything takes quite a bit of effort.

Take device management. While consumers once had one, maybe two, devices on which to receive media, today that number has mushroomed. Consumers may now have multiple televisions, multiple computers both at home and at work, a device for storing downloaded music, another for mobile calls, a game console, multiple e-mail accounts—and that's not to mention the old-fashioned stuff still hanging around, like the telephone. This army of devices creates its own mini-drama. Consumers must keep track of them, manage them, charge them, learn their features and their quirks, worry about them when they fail to function as expected, and fret that each one, however new it may be, is already obsolete and overtaken by the Next Big Thing.

Content overload is also a problem. Not only do consumers have more screens to look at, but also those screens are spouting more content than ever imagined. Consumers have access to scheduled programming, online extras, live chats, e-mail newsletters, message forums, and RSS feeds. That's just a few. To keep up, multitasking has become a way of life. The vast majority of consumers say that while watching television, they also read the newspaper and go online. While online, consumers say they often watch television, listen to the radio, or read the paper. Simultaneously reading the paper, listening to the radio, and watching television is often commonplace. BIGresearch shows that consumers experience media in multitudes of two and three; 70% of Web users say they watch TV occasionally to regularly while they surf. Newspaper readers say they watch TV occasionally to regularly while they read, and 51% of radio listeners occasionally to regularly read the newspaper while listening.[5] Yet there are still only 24 hours in the day. It's not easy, even for empowered consumers, to keep up with the demands of the media market. The result: a state of mind I call MAD—media attention disorder. And it is rampant among empowered consumers, racing to stay ahead of the surging technology tide.

Faced with these demanding, tech-savvy, busy individuals, how can you best present your wares? Several key points must be addressed.

The first is speed. If empowered consumers will abandon a Web page because it loads too slowly, that's a key metric for any advertiser to embrace. Messages of all kinds must be quick. Requiring consumers to slog through a lot of copy, sit through a long setup, or wait, really for anything at all, is a tremendous risk. These are consumers weaned on fast information, and advertising must comply or find itself bypassed.

Speed takes many forms—certainly, in the content of the ad itself. Pitches must be focused, on point, and immediately clear to the recipients. Consumers who are multitasking between three media options will have only limited attention for your ad coming across on any one device. You have seconds before that eyeball flicks away, before that trigger finger zips past your ad to the next media option. Your message must be fast to be received.

Speed plays an additional role in the creation and roll out of campaigns. While it was once possible to spend months researching, testing, and rolling out a campaign or product to consumers, today, that window of opportunity has been greatly reduced. The evidence of this need for speed is all around us. By the time music device rivals realized what Apple was doing, iPod was already an icon of an era. Hollywood now concedes that if a movie is not a hit in its opening weekend, the game is over. New TV shows, once allowed to "find an audience," are now off the air if early ratings are lackluster. A product or service must find an audience with speed unthinkable in generations past. In today's technology-driven world, those who hesitate are lost.

Besides quick, an ad must be versatile. Creating a campaign that works on one device only limits your potential audience. Consider again the multitaskers, toggling mightily across two and three devices at a time. Now consider how effective your pitch might be if it could live on more than one screen. What's more is that even if you're satisfied with one-screen advertising, consumers are not. Today's empowered consumers want to access advertising on their own terms, and that means on their device of choice. What new movies are opening this weekend? Consumers may watch television one week to find out, log on to a Web site the next for similar information, and use a PDA to download the data some other time. The messages must be available on the device the consumers have in hand at the time. In the old days, marketers decided on a media platform. Today, consumers make the call, and advertisers must flex with that demand mindset.

Ultimately, empowered consumers raise the bar for advertising quality. When consumers had no choice in the matter, advertisers could get away with sloppy advertising. It could be weak in its creative, fuzzy in its focus, even stretching the bounds of truth and accuracy. Consumers had little recourse.

Today, that's simply not true. Accuracy in advertising is essential—empowered consumers are one click away from unmasking any little white lies. Attempts to inflate, exaggerate, or aggrandize will be swiftly debunked—and the attempt made widely public.

In the same vein, advertising must be relevant. This has always been a mantra of the industry, but empowered consumers give it more pressing status. In the old days, irrelevant advertising might mean fewer sales. Today, it means your ad gets zapped, perhaps in seconds. This recasts the concept of the mass-market advertising campaign. Can a mass campaign be relevant to all viewers? Perhaps advertisers will need to forgo mass for a series of more targeted pitches.

Finally, advertising must be entertaining. For all the seriousness with which empowered consumers approach their lives, ads, they maintain, must entertain. They must be funny or poignant or exciting. They must be noteworthy, rising to a level that befits attention from the MAD consumers. An ad that does not entertain holds little hope of breaking through the media forest to its target consumers. There is too much already in front of consumers that is entertaining. An ad that is not is shut out.

There's some fear that empowered consumers mean a less profitable ad industry. But leading-edge experts suggest that this is a false concern. Consider the comments of Tim Armstrong, vice president of advertising sales at Google:

> "The fearful conventional wisdom says the advertising world cannot help but shrink in the era of the empowered consumer. But what's the flip side of this fear? When advertising took place on media companies' schedules, a marketer's job was to deliver one-way messages designed to build strong brands. Coke showed us emotional commercials, and if we wanted more data about its products than an image of people singing on a hill, we were out of luck. Learning to sell to empowered consumers means moving from 'the brand is the product' to 'the product is the brand.' In a TiVo universe whose inhabitants can turn off unwanted messages at any moment, marketers must understand and communicate product benefits and attributes in a way that earns potential customers' trust and meets their needs."[6]

The rise of empowered consumers has different implications for different sections of the industry.

For agencies, empowered consumers require a shift in overall mindset. Call it the shift from analog to digital thinking. While advertising once was constructed and delivered via analog rules, empowered consumers must be contacted using digital rules. In the analog world, consumers were passive, but in the digital world, they are active. In analog, advertising was pushed to consumers. Under digital rules, the advertising is pulled in by consumers. Analog advertising functioned in distinct media silos—television was separate from print, which was separate from radio. There was some coordination to keep all the elements under a common thematic umbrella, but these media silos functioned with a great deal of autonomy. In the digital world, media have converged and so too must the messaging coming from agencies. A pitch must live not in one silo but across devices, finding empowered consumers whenever they decide to lean forward and pull the message in.

It is the difference, ultimately, between interruption and invitation. Under the old rules, advertising was by design an interruption in the content delivery process. The goal was to make that interruption as attractive as possible. Today, the advertisers aren't in a position to interrupt anything. Consumers hold the technology and the power to control any and all contact. Interruption is a lot harder than it used to be. So a new stance must be adopted by agencies: one of invitation. Consumers can't be forced into advertising contact. They must be enticed.

Finally, while the analog world was comfortable using targeted marketing—for example, crafting messages by demographic group or region—the new world of digital marketing demands far more precision. The mass market is rapidly becoming a thing of the past. It's the era of one-to-one marketing, and newly demanding consumers will judge a pitch on just how narrowly relevant it can be. The more individualized the pitch is, the more impact it will have with consumers.

Today's buyers expect that level of service and will choose media, products, and services based upon who can provide it. Agencies will need to step up and offer guidance, talent, and services that speak to this new reality.

Media are already undergoing the transformation. The collection of traditional media—television, print, and radio—is being replaced by the buffet of new options. Today's advertisers need options on all of the new platforms, including digital cable, online, wireless, and out of home. Media companies are already working to cope with the fragmentation.

But fragmentation is not media's only challenge. The seismic changes brought to the consumer experience have done more than remake the process of advertising. Media must also adjust to the new economics of the industry. As more and more consumers enter the state of MAD, the competition for their attention becomes more and more fierce. Under the old system, advertisers determined how much money would be allocated to media out of the total marketing budget. It was a system that was dollar centric. But now, the focus has shifted. The new paradigm is attention centric. Media are competing for the attention of consumers, and advertisers will need to start paying not for impressions but for attention. Human attention is a scarce resource in the empowered consumer marketplace. It can no longer be taken for granted.

Advertisers must alter their expectations—and their willingness to try new tactics. They must be willing to branch out from traditional media and try new formats. They'll need to look to new formats, such as branded entertainment, that allow them to get in front of consumers without being skipped or zapped by the latest technology. Advertisers will need to embrace the fact that consumers now feel empowered to interact with advertising. Flexible campaigns that encourage consumer participation will become more popular, and companies brave enough to let consumers customize their brands will reap rewards. Advertisers will need to understand the new economics of the marketing world—one that is measured in human attention rather than marketing dollars. And most important, they'll have to be willing to follow their emboldened customers into these new arenas of digital possibilities. The command and control once wielded by advertisers have been usurped by consumers armed with the latest in technology. That power shift is a reality. Advertisers will need to adjust accordingly.

Pleasing Empowered Consumers: A checklist for advertisers

Once in the power position, advertisers now find themselves working for very demanding new clients: empowered consumers. Armed with high expectations and customizable technology, the consumers are taking old assumptions and flipping them upside down. Advertisers must now review all aspects of messaging to conform to the demands of this new consumer mindset. How can you know whether you're connecting? To get in with today's empowered consumers, you need to be sure your program passes muster. Consider this checklist: The Four C's.

Content: First and foremost, any communication you make with empowered consumers must meet high standards for content. Is it funny? Thrilling? Visually gripping? Dramatic? Informative? If it's less than high quality, it will fall flat. Consumers evaluate advertising using the same standards they apply to entertainment content. If your content is weak, your ad is in peril. The attention of consumers is limited to superior content—whatever format it may take.

Choice: There is no "one size fits all" in the world of empowered consumers. Advertisers, agencies, and media must be prepared to offer choices: choices in product, choices in time and place of the retail experience, choices in how and when an ad is delivered.

Customization: In a world where no two phones ring the same, consumers are used to a high level of customization. Products, services, and advertising must be flexible enough to meet these demands. Empowered consumers will gravitate to a message that invites interactivity rather than passivity.

Convenience: Appointment television is fast approaching relic status and so too is the concept that advertisers decide when their ads will be viewed. Empowered consumers aren't averse to viewing advertising, but it has to happen on their schedule, not that of the corporate community. Ads must be available for enjoyment at the discretion of the user and on the device of choice. Convenience is not an extra; it's the price of entry for today's consumers.

Six

Advertising and Politics

Quick—name the world's most famous political TV ad. That's an easy one. No serious student of American politics will miss the reference to the "Daisy Girl" ad, the TV spot created in support of Lyndon B. Johnson's 1964 presidential campaign. It was a masterful act of creative. The ad starts with a little girl playing with a daisy—the picture of childhood innocence. She is counting her flower petals when suddenly another voice overtakes hers. It is a countdown to a missile blastoff. The lovely Daisy is threatened by the evil specter of nuclear war. The final image: the unmistakable mushroom cloud.

It was a soul-gripping, stomach-dropping moment in the American consciousness. Millions know about the ad, can describe it accurately, and understand its storied role in the American political landscape.

Not bad for an ad that aired only once. "Daisy," the best-known political ad ever made, had only one paid run on American television. The airing of "Daisy" was a national story overnight. Critics of LBJ blasted the campaign for its bare-knuckle scare tactics. Supporters challenged Goldwater campaign backers to face the reality of the issues in the campaign. The ad was pulled as a paid spot as the campaign and TV networks reacted, buckling to the complaints of ordinary viewers who were unaccustomed to being scared to pieces by a TV ad. However, that did not matter. Daisy never again had to pay for ad time. She was aired free, repeatedly, by the eager news media.

Indeed, she continues to see airtime today, more than 40 years after the election that made her famous ended.

Daisy is just one example of how the industries of politics and advertising function in a state of symbiosis. While marketers of consumer products and other goods and services may be questioning their ad spends, political and social causes continue to look for new ways to pour more money into ad platforms. The campaign industry is a bright spot for advertising. It is one that is growing and in no danger of shrinking any time soon. It is an industry expanding into new media while not forsaking older formats. It is an industry that still depends heavily on advertising to get the message to the American public. From traditional television to emerging new media, the bond between politics and advertising is strong.

When it comes to old media, politics has few complaints. Television remains a powerful platform for reaching the American voter. In 2005, political candidates and advocacy groups spent more than $560 million pitching the American voter, and most of that money went to television.[1]

In 2005, Michael Bloomberg put $36 million—much of it his own money from his personal fortune—into his campaign against challenger Fernando Ferrer. The ads touted the improvements in New York City's public schools, the stronger economy of the city, and the recovery of New York since 9-11. Ferrer, a longtime New York democrat, spent $7 million telling voters he could do better. Bloomberg won by a landslide.[2]

That same year, Jon Corzine battled Doug Forrester for the right to be the governor of the State of New Jersey. The ads stretched far beyond the campaign issues and in the final weeks dissolved into an ugly mudslinging contest that grew louder and nastier as election day approached. Corzine spent $37 million to Forrester's $30 million.[3] Corzine won the day.

Television ads work even when there is not a candidate on the ballot. In 2005, Governor Arnold Schwarzenegger launched an aggressive series of ballot initiatives by framing them as his reform agenda. They ranged in topics from teacher tenure to union dues. Eight items faced California voters that year. More than $90 million was spent on TV advertising in California's top five media markets. Groups that opposed the governor's initiatives outspent him two to one. Not a single initiative passed. At a time when television is under attack, the medium has found supporters in the ranks of the candidates and advocacy groups. Television ads are an integral part of the election process.

How did this happen? The trend has many feeders. However, the biggest impact can be traced to Washington, D.C. The Bipartisan Campaign Reform Act of 2002, also known as the McCain-Feingold Bill, after its primary sponsors, released a flood of new money available to political campaigns. The legislation designed to bring ethics and responsibility to the electoral fund-raising process has generated a boom in ad funds.

The old campaign laws had long capped the amount individuals could give at $1,000 per election. McCain-Feingold doubled this to $2,000 for each election. That move uncovered an interesting pricing dynamic among American voters. Far from being put off by the higher ceiling, contributors rose to it. Turns out individuals willing to contribute $1,000 were not at all unwilling to contribute $2,000. The doubling of individual contributions was felt immediately. For example, a senate campaign once armed with an $8 million budget had a $15 million budget, close to double. And because the cost of running a campaign had remained relatively steady, that extra money flowed easily into the advertising budget.

Individual contributions were not the only source of new money. McCain-Feingold also failed to close the loophole for outside money and left a back door for what have come to be known in the industry as 527s. Additionally, other tax-exempt advocacy groups like 501c3s and other member organizations could exploit these same loopholes to advocate the election or defeat of candidates. These nonprofit advocacy groups' primary purpose became to collect money and run political ads. Between the doubled contributions and the primed and ready 527s, the political arena experienced an injection of new advertising money—and these were only the high-profile funding sources. A look at the complex machinery of campaign funding shows many moving parts. For example, the Bush for President campaign drew funding from the Republican National Committee (RNC) and issue groups such as Progress for America and what came to be known as the Swift Boat Veterans for Truth. It also had many other smaller funding sources, such as Americans United to Preserve Marriage, the Republican Party of Florida, and the National Rifle Association. The Kerry campaign amassed a similar collection of funding sources. The Democratic National Committee, MoveOn.org, and the American Federation of Labor–Congress of Industrial Unions (AFL-CIO) led the pack; along with the United Auto Workers and the National Abortion and Reproductive Rights Action League.

Why does this money go to television? The small screen serves a big purpose. The truth is that politicians are a product like no other. While the brand manager for Pepsi may spend years marketing, strategizing, and sparring with soft drink opponents, the campaign manager doesn't have that kind of luxury. Most products have time and space in which to maneuver. Politicians have one day in which they must attract more than 50% of available consumers or the game is over. Imagine for a moment that you sell dog food. Instead of having weeks or months to woo your consumer and build your business, you have to convince more than half of your market to buy your product on one and only one sales day. The "one-day winner-takes-all" nature of politics means that many interesting, creative, and thoughtful forms of advertising are simply unworkable. The slow build of the newspaper print campaign takes too long. The four-color spread of the magazine requires a long lead time and doesn't allow for flexibility.

Television, by contrast, is well suited to politics. It can be local or national. It can be constant or infrequent. It can deliver information, emotion, or both with searing intensity. It can start with just a few spots that build to a blitz by election day. It can be customized to react to an opponent's charges. It can be standardized and shown across multiple markets in an identical format. It is the one ad distribution mechanism capable of keeping up with the rough and tumble of American politics. What's more is that the medium continues to improve its return on investment for political customers. Why?

THE MEDIA LOVE POLITICAL ADS

Daisy was the first media darling to come up out of the political arena. Because she caused such a stir, other campaigns sought to create their own controversial ads in the hopes that they too would generate hours of news coverage. It worked. In the Reagan Era, "It's Morning in America" and "The Bear" drew news coverage. Michael Dukakis was undone in part by repeated news coverage of an ad that criticized his views on parole. "Willie Horton" was a household name, even in households that never saw the ad as a paid spot. The Bush and Kerry campaigns produced their own media stars, from ads that featured wolf packs, Osama bin Laden, and news footage from the Vietnam era. Ads that focused on Kerry's service in Vietnam were run in paid spots in key markets, but they saw airtime all over the country once the media picked them up as newsworthy. All were treated as news stories throughout the campaign and saw hundreds of free airings in the course of political coverage. The use of ads as fodder for news stories has only increased as news coverage has moved to a 24/7 schedule. Now, broadcast and cable networks are constantly hungry for campaign news, and clever, gripping, controversial ads are just the ticket to keep viewers engaged. Their appetite for the newsworthy ad has grown and shows no signs of abating.

THE NEW AGE OF BRACKETING

The improved targeting marketers can achieve through Customer Relationship Management (CRM) in the consumer products world is increasingly available for guiding choices in political TV advertising. Once, campaigns relied on ratings data to guide their media buys, but today there is a lot more information available. Research can now tell campaign managers more than just basic demographic information. Now that profiles can be fleshed out, who are your target voters? What are their favorite magazines, Web sites, and TV and radio shows? What other media do they consume? All that information can be had, and it makes buying TV time that much smarter.

Campaign experts call the process "bracketing," and the Bush and Kerry campaigns made smart work of it during the presidential election. Instead of buying TV time based on ratings, the campaigns bought spots based on the TV consumption habits of their target voters. The ads followed voters through the day, turning up on their favorite morning news shows, their favorite evening sports contests, and their late-night comics of choice. The ads surrounded the voters and took their ad experiences from a scant 30 seconds to an all-day running theme. Ads targeting Republican voters in 17 key states turned up on shows such as *American Idol* and *America's Most Wanted*. Ads reaching out to Kerry voters turned up on *Dr. Phil*, *Joan of Arcadia*, and *The Price Is Right*. The strategy: surround voters throughout the day.

Another new way to use television is micro-targeting. While campaigns will spend the most money at the end and saturate a market, micro-targeting allows them to be more focused and make smarter, smaller ad buys early in the season. This is a critical improvement. It allows campaigns to leverage the power of television at a time when many voters may still be undecided. This is a more efficient use of the TV budget and a way to effectively pitch to voters who may be on the fence in any given campaign. Before these tactics, campaigns were forced to pay for the widest possible net of TV advertising, even as they knew that some of it was going to waste on voters who had already made up their minds. Bracketed and micro-targeted ads, on the other hand, put the money to smarter, more effective use.

THE DIGITAL EDGE

Finally, there is one more very good reason why political ads will only become more prevalent on television. It is because they are cheap.

That was not always the case. Time in a high-quality TV ad was something only the mega-candidates could afford. The combined cost of production, airtime, and creative and media expertise ran easily into the tens of thousands of dollars. Ads made on the cheap were obvious in their shortcomings. Few candidates were willing to look bad with a shoddy ad. As a result, many campaigns took their hard-won war chest elsewhere.

The digital revolution has remade the ad making business. Technology has brought efficiency and ease to what was once an expensive and complicated project. What was once a five-figure extravaganza is now something many can manage with a good how-to book and $3,000 worth of digital equipment. The new lower cost of making an ad has opened the process to many more campaigners. Once, TV ads were only for national and well-financed state candidates. Today, almost anyone can make a decent-looking TV ad at a reasonable price. Therefore, almost everyone is making them. Candidates for local magistrate, county coroner, and dogcatcher can all afford to make and air TV spots, further buttressing television's status as the premier political ad platform. It is where everyone wants to be to reach the American voter.

NEW TECHNOLOGY

Still, even as television reigns as the format of choice for American politics, new technology is ready to give television a run for the political ad budget. New media has captured the imagination of both the candidates and the voters, and elections are beginning to reflect the impact. The 2004 presidential race was notable not just for the candidates who fought to the finish line but also for those who never got out of the primaries. First among the losers was Howard Dean. Dean may not have won his race, but he left his mark on the industry. He gave us a glimpse of how the Internet may be emerging as the new media darling of politicians.

The dawn of the new millennium was marked by a considered focus on the virtual world. The political industry was gripped by the possibilities of new technology. Leadership hustled to be the first to leverage these new tactics. "In the wake of the 2000 election, each political party, convinced that its opponent was getting ahead, stepped up its investments in technology and information gathering."[4]

Indeed, Howard Dean made his run for the Democratic nomination by using an organizational strategy that relied on the Internet to advance his message, grow his supporter lists, and, most important, raise what Senator Phil Gramm once called the "mother's milk" of politics—money. Dean, a likable doctor and the former governor of Vermont, used a team of Internet-savvy message moguls to stake out a seemingly suicidal position of opposing the war in Iraq. In the post-9-11 era, this was a huge gamble. However, it paid off for Dean. As the war effort in Iraq became bogged down, he was able to capitalize. He offered a steady, sober, hopeful message and promised withdrawal from the increasingly dismal conflict, and he was a hit. He was able to raise vast amounts of money, one click at a time.

When his message began to gain traction and a new group of younger anti-war voters began to donate enough money to make Dean a relevant front-runner in the Democratic Party, the bigger checks followed as party bigwigs hustled to cover their bases and show support for the new man of the hour in the Democratic primary. Dean began to appear on television in advertising and in news coverage. He bought spots and time in markets such as Washington, New York, and even Bush's territory in Austin, Texas, a move that provided his campaign with a great deal of news coverage and earned media in the normally news-void summer. He turned up as a guest on the popular Sunday morning talk shows. He was interviewed by all the major traditional media. Nevertheless, the base of his marketing machine remained in the virtual world. He raised money and support by using e-mail blasts, blogs, and other virtual communications. He was a phenomenon of the medium—the first true national Internet candidate.

Dean failed to grab his party's nomination. Indeed, Kerry took the day in part by pouring his cash into TV ads in Iowa. But the Dean campaign did accomplish a key goal: it awakened the industry to the possibilities of the Internet. Headed into the next national contest, those lessons are playing out. In 2006, candidates trekked to digital media conferences to pitch their messages to the nation's top bloggers—a clear nod to the power the Internet holds. Studies cropped up showing that the voting public now embraces the Internet as a key conduit of political information. In 2005, almost 40% of Internet users agreed that going online could give people more political power. That was up from 27% in the pervious year. What's more is that 61.7% agreed that the online world is critical to political campaigns.[5] The same study, conducted by the Center for the Digital Future at the University of Southern California (USC) Annenberg School, showed that more than three-quarters of those who go online for political information are undecided at the time they log on.[6] In other words, they are prime candidates for a political message. They are hand raisers. They want to know more. Increasingly, political campaigns will be online to give the people what they want.

Going forward, both new and old media can expect more political ad money.

THE RISE OF THE PERMANENT CAMPAIGN

There was a time when campaigns had a narrowly defined season. You took to the streets during your election year, in your election season, and you made your pitch to the American voters in an agreed-upon slice of time and ad space. But in recent years, candidates and campaigns have been unwilling to stick to that traditional script and have pushed the bounds of the campaign season by making it more of an ongoing event.

President Bill Clinton and his campaign get some credit for this trend. In his 1996 bid for reelection, he did not wait until after the convention to begin his ad blitz. Instead, he ran what has come to be known as the "stealth campaign," running issue ads in battleground states all through the late spring and summer of that year. By the time convention season rolled around in July and August, Clinton's TV ads had been seen by millions of voters in the battleground or swing states. Even before the start of traditional campaigning, hearts and minds had been influenced and won. The ad season had been stretched to almost double its original length. It was a turning point in American politics.

That was just the beginning of the amazing expanding campaign season. If 2005 showed anything, it demonstrated the power or myth of the "off" year. Even without a presidential race on the near-term calendar, political ads were still on the air in droves. TNS-MI/Campaign Media Analysis Group captured 453,000 ad airings that year. More than two dozen races scheduled for 2006 bought airtime in 2005 to get the ball rolling. Between races and issue advertising, a record $560 million was spent on TV ads, as the medium remained the key vehicle for communicating political messages.[7] Rick Klein of *The Boston Globe* reported:

> "The Democrats' project is being considered a new benchmark in the trend toward 'permanent campaigns' which specialists said is transforming the political culture."[8]

What used to be downtime in the political ad business has heated up to new heights. Candidates have learned to campaign early and often.

YOU DON'T NEED A CANDIDATE

Who says political advertising is just for politicians? Along with the permanent campaign has emerged a new trend, what's being called the "culture of advocacy." That culture marshals the agendas and ad budgets of special interest groups and keeps them spinning their political machines even when there is no race to be run. The cast of characters is vast; it encompasses the 527s and issues groups, corporations, and the ever-burgeoning class of associations.

These are groups that have a stake in politics, whether or not there is an election at stake. Companies eager to influence the course of events in Washington spend on TV advertising, and they are making the most of their airtime. Whether it's General Electric depicting an elephant singing in the rain to sell clean coal technology or a pharmaceutical company touting its latest discovery to prevent price controls or new patent laws, all flock to television to make their stands known, election year or not. And the 527s don't take the off years off either. They simply raise more money and march out in support or opposition of the latest sexy issue. Now a fixture in the American political conversation, they don't need a candidate to make their message known. They will happily advertise in the candidate-free zone of the off year.

GOING FORWARD

What is ahead for the marriage of politics and advertising? Early evidence suggests more banner years.

Projections put 2006 ad spending at well over $1.5 billion, possibly topping 2004's record totals. Nearly half the gubernatorial races and 40% of the Senate races are considered "in play," forecasting a strong advertising market. Early primary spending in states such as Texas, New York, California, and Illinois hit $57 million in the early part of the year.[9] And historically, more than 80% of spending happens in the last 60 days of a campaign.

The 2006 push by Democrats to retake control of the U.S. House of Representatives is expected to be the most aggressive campaign series since 1998. More seats than ever are in play, and that will bring the ad money out in force.

State lawmakers and issue advocates will continue to leverage ballot initiatives to engage the attention of the voting public. Nearly $100 million was spent in the early months of 2006 on issue ads run by state and federal followers of telecom, tort reform, and health care.[10] The 527s are expected to be active in the in play races on the state and federal levels. In the 2006 campaigns, third-party spending is expected to top 2004 levels.

The 2008 presidential campaign is expected to break records in terms of its length and overall cost. In addition to the national campaign, several key states have governor's races in 2008, further stoking the political ad climate.

All of that is good news for TV advertising. In 2004, only 9% of political and issue ad spending was on media outside of broadcast television, and that percentage is not expected to shift markedly in the next election cycle.[11]

However, fascination with new media will continue in political circles, especially as media become more portable and the Web more prevalent in American life. That will bring increased attention—and advertising dollars—to the Internet.

What does the future hold? Already, politics is showing its willingness to learn the tactics of new media. In elections ahead, look for political campaigns to try many of the bells and whistles that are now in the early stages of consumer marketing.

Some campaigns are blazing the trail. Experts say the 2004 South Dakota race for senate, won by John Thune, was influenced by an online ad featuring Rudy Giuliani. The ad recorded more click-throughs than the number of votes that decided the election. In the 2004 Los Angeles race for mayor, candidate Bob Herzberg saw his polling numbers bounce after he began pushing his plan to divide the Los Angeles school district—a plan he promoted heavily via online ads.[12]

Advocacy groups are also moving toward the digital future. Vote Latino, a youth voter registration organization aimed at Latino youths, has teamed up with Mobile Voter, a San Francisco nonprofit dedicated to harnessing the power of text messaging and mobile technology. Their goal: to register at least 35,000 Hispanic youths to vote nationwide using Mobile Voter services. Once that channel is open, what's to stop the flow of additional political messages via the smallest screen?[13]

Today, cutting-edge campaigns are using these tools—online ads, e-mail, text messages, and blogs—to reach target voters. But there is much more on the drawing board. Consider a future in which one-to-one marketing comes to the campaign trail. Office seekers may use contextual advertising to reach voters with messages at key moments. For example, a potential voter may be doing a search on a particular campaign issue keyword or for a political candidate. That action could trigger the delivery of a whole set of ads focused on that topic or candidate. Or perhaps the opposition could use the moment to interject its own side of the political story. Either way, the ad is delivered at the moment at which the potential voter is considering his or her options on Election Day.

Behavioral advertising could also be leveraged in a political context. By tapping into data stores of consumer behavior, campaigns could conceivably target their messaging based not just on basic demographics but also on a detailed subset of search behavior. The possibility for voter engagement is enormous. In this more targeted political ad world, campaigns could craft their messages to be specific to a voter's experience rather than relying on the broader messaging used in most TV ads.

The one-to-one political advertising world is not without its dark side. Unlike TV campaigns and other high-profile marketing methods, a one-to-one ad campaign, triggered by individualized behavior, is less open to scrutiny. The messaging that appears on a single screen during a search is hard for outsiders to monitor.

Also, the Internet, while gaining popularity, is still not as widely used as television. Computer access is on the rise, but television is the medium with nearly 100% penetration in American households. A candidate relying on new media risks missing the voters still relying on the old.

The evolution will bring with it its own set of challenges. Says Jeffery I. Cole, director of the Center for the Digital Future at the USC Annenberg School:

> "The Internet is providing a direct conduit through which office seekers can reach voters without media gatekeepers sifting and interpreting politicians' messages. This issue raises many questions. While the Internet creates an open forum for delivery of information, it can be used just as easily for responsible campaigning or as a platform for political mischief and miscommunication. How will the growing role of the Internet shape political campaigns of elections to come?"[14]

The answer: by joining with traditional media and maintaining the steady stream of messaging to American voters.

Seven

The Future of Agencies

The 2006 upfront season went off as it has for years. Networks presented their slate of programming. Media buyers set about negotiating. The parties argued over prices, strategies, politics, and the effect of new technology. And in the end, it was déjà vu all over again. Billions of dollars—the lion's share of industry funds—went to place ads on network television. It was business as usual—and that's a big problem for the industry. Because while the world is changing at an unprecedented pace, the advertising industry is going through many of the same old motions, over and over again.

Nowhere is that resistance to change more obvious than in the advertising agencies. Responsible for the creative, the media decisions, and much of the advice given to major marketers about their brands and messaging, agencies are uniquely front and center in this debate over change and tradition.

In many ways, ad agencies know that this is a problem. Said Ron Berger, CEO and chief creative officer of Euro RSCG Worldwide, outgoing AAAA chairman at the 2006 AAAA Management Conference for Agency CEOs: "I think our industry would be better if agencies were as comfortable with change as we like to tell clients they should be."

But as a group, they are not. The American Advertising Federation opened its 2006 conference with the news that 90% of its members see opportunity in the digital world, but 58% admitted they had problems keeping up with the pace of change. Two-thirds of those in the survey said the industry's biggest companies were "generally behind the curve" in the new media environment. Two-thirds again underscored the upfront experience: there was little change in the way they were spending on network television.[1]

Even as the world shifts around them, many agencies continue to lead their clients into the traditional combinations of television, print, radio, and outdoor. They continue to develop ads that consumers tell us they are skipping or zapping or using as time to go to the kitchen and make a sandwich. They continue to go through the motions that have been standard for decades and look to markers such as day parts and ratings to guide decision making. They continue to embrace the calendar as a road map. It is a steady, familiar behavior. It brings to mind the old adage about how to get ahead on Wall Street. "No one ever got fired for buying IBM."

But that adage isn't true on Wall Street anymore, and agencies too must lose their risk-averse positioning.

It's understandable that agencies feel this way. After all, the nature of the business puts them in a precarious position. They are only as good as their last campaign, and clients have shown a frightening lack of loyalty in the past decade. While the partnership between agency and client was once one for a generation, today it is a year-to-year, even a quarter-to-quarter, arrangement. With that much to lose, agencies are loath to advise anything risky, newfangled, or dangerous. If it goes badly, the agency can expect to be kicked to the curb with all due speed.

Still, somehow, the agency community must find a way to evolve with the times—because the times are not waiting around. Consider for a moment the activity in April 2006 at the U.S. Patent and Trademark Office. This is the government's entity designed expressly to promote and protect creative discoveries. Its sole mission is to support and reward innovation.

Now, look closely at the numbers:

- Since 1790, there were 27,311 issued patents that mention "advertising."

- Out of these 27,311 patents, 24,114 were issued since 1976.
- From 2000 to 2006, there were 10,647 issued patents that mention "advertising."
- Since 2001, there were 20,483 published patents pending that mention "advertising."

These numbers support the theory that innovation affecting the advertising industry is rapidly increasing.

But where is this innovation coming from? Going back to the patent office records, another pattern emerges. Patent holders and applicants within the advertising industry (whose innovations have the primary purpose of affecting the advertising industry) are more likely to include "advertising" in the title and/or abstract. At the same time, patent holders and applicants outside the industry (whose innovations have a secondary effect on the advertising industry) are less likely to include "advertising" in the title and/or abstract but rather mention "advertising" in the general description. Knowing that, look at these numbers:

- Out of the 27,311 issued patents that mention "advertising" since 1790, there are 2,710 that include "advertising" in the title and 1,789 that include "advertising" in the abstract.
- Out of the 24,114 issued patents that mention "advertising" since 1976, there are 800 that include "advertising" in the title and 1,962 that include "advertising" in the abstract.
- Out of the 10,647 issued patents that mention "advertising" from 2000 to 2006, there are 329 that include "advertising" in the title and 748 that include "advertising" in the abstract.
- Out of the 20,483 published patents pending since 2001, there are 913 that include "advertising" in the title and 1,999 that mention "advertising" in the abstract.

These numbers support the theory that innovation affecting the advertising industry is occurring from sources outside the industry itself. Agencies are not the sources of what is on the cutting edge of the advertising world. Ad agencies have never put themselves forth as technologists, but they will have to find a way to be a part of this trend. If technology companies and other firms outside of traditional advertising circles are producing the most innovative ideas in the advertising world, agencies will need to co-opt these ideas, through partnerships, vendor relationships, and joint ventures and even in the creation of new in-house departments and areas of expertise. Innovation is out there, and agencies need to harness it.

Are agencies on their way out? Hardly. They are still the core repositories of talent, vision, and institutional memory for the industry. What's more is that clients want them to stick around. No marketer wants to take on this responsibility in house. Often, when you approach a major marketer with an advertising concept or opportunity, the response will be "My agency handles that; here's how to get in touch with someone there." Clients want their agencies to step up and lead the way. They do not want the burden and responsibility of creating and managing their own ad campaign. But at the same time, they are holding agencies to a higher standard. Agencies will have to evolve in order to function in the new digital reality.

BOOST CREATIVITY

In the age of empowered consumers, there is no room for dull advertising. The consumers simply won't stand for it. When consumers are armed with the remote control, the DVR, and the pop-up blocker, uninteresting ads are history. Even if they manage to avoid the technical hurdles, busy consumers have only so much attention to devote. Today's consumers are often toggling between two or three media at a time: watching television while reading a magazine, listening to music while commuting to work, reading the newspaper with the radio on. The competition for attention is intense. If your ad is not flat out the most eye-catching, interest-holding item of any given moment, it's not going to get even 30 seconds of precious consumer attention.

The response to this problem is not to block the technology but to be sure that advertising clears the higher hurdles set by empowered consumers. Ads simply have to be better, more engaging, more entertaining, and worthy competitors to the other content available today.

Every year, the Super Bowl rolls around, and the debate kicks up in the industry as to whether these ads are "worth it." That's a cringeworthy argument. Are they "worth it?" Of course they are—and the industry needs more of them. Every year, millions of consumers make appointments to sit and watch several hours of advertising. They'll include it in their party plans. They'll hush the rest of the room when the ads come on. They'll give the ads their undivided attention as they run and discuss them even when the 30 or 60 seconds are over. We don't need less of this kind of eye-catching, attention-grabbing, engaging advertising. We need more of it, and agencies need to stop looking at this as special-occasion work. That level of entertainment needs to happen far more than once a year. It needs to be the new normal in the industry. Consumers show every year on Super Bowl Sunday that they are willing to plan entire afternoons around good advertising. Agencies need to step up to that opening and deliver entertainment in ad format.

In addition to being more entertaining, advertising needs to be less unpleasant. It's hard to believe that has to be stated, but frankly, agencies are far too lax when it comes to pumping out advertising and ad formats the consumer has flat out rejected as objectionable. Take pop-up ads. Consumers don't like them. They say they don't like them. They tell the opinion pollsters, the forums and message boards, their friends and family, everyone, that they don't like them. And yet, the agency community, from creatives to media buyers, continues to use that format. How does that make any sense? Agencies need to create work served in formats consumers like.

Some ad experts will argue that consumers don't have to like an ad for it to be effective. This is old-fashioned thinking. Perhaps that was true in past eras, when consumers had little choice but to endure whatever ads were set before them. Today, that's not a requirement. Consumers can easily avoid an ad that annoys them. They can buy software to block it, they can use other technology to avoid it, and they can choose alternative content that serves up more appealing advertising. Consumers have choices. Agencies can't risk annoying them with formats they hate.

In addition to being creative in content, agencies will need to be creative in delivery. Agencies are very used to the standard formats: 30-second spots in commercials, four-color layouts in magazines, column inches in newspapers. But boosting the creativity has to come to the delivery of the ads as well as their content. How else can that message get to the consumer? Can it be woven into the content? Can it be e-mailed? Blogged? Wrapped around the outside of a bus? Mowed into the grass at Yankee Stadium? Agencies need to shrug off the confines of the previous era and bring an element of creativity to the full spectrum of their offerings.

It's true: in the old days, nobody ever got fired for buying IBM. But the era of big blue, and the staid blue-chip economy it represented, is over. Creativity is happening in the advertising world. Agencies need to embrace this thinking, not just in their advice to clients but also in their own workdays.

EMBRACE THE DIGITAL REALITY

While agencies may be discussing the shift from an analog to a digital experience, consumers are racing ahead. Broadband use is booming, expected to reach 69.4 million households by 2008—a 100% increase from 2004.[2] The media habits of consumers are changing, and the shift is only going to become more dramatic as the next generation, the one raised on this technology, comes into its prime spending years.

For evidence, see the May 2006 survey of teenagers from Burst Media. Two-thirds of kids ages 13 to 17 said that going 24 hours without Web access would be a hardship. Nearly 40% said they spend three hours or more per day on the Internet, and another 18% spend two to three hours online.[3] That's a big shift from the average adult user, who spends just over two hours online per day.[4] Another hallmark of the digital age: teens are often media multitasking. So they are watching television and surfing the Internet or listening to music while playing video games. This creates an even greater challenge for agencies. Not only must they create ads that function on digital platforms, but also they must wrestle with the reality that has digital consumers constantly flitting from screen to screen. Digital advances have made history of the captive audience. Consumers now navigate a wide variety of media and machines throughout the day. For agencies, that means embracing not just new technology but also the new digital lifestyle.

Says Chuck Moran, manager of market research at Burst Media:

> "Regardless of media type, I think advertisers are going to have a tough time getting through to teens if they don't consider all the touch points they have into teens' lives. I made the point that teens are 'media multi-taskers,' but I don't think simultaneously using various technologies or media types has to be disruptive from a marketing perspective. Teens are a savvy segment and use technologies and media as complements to one another. The smart marketer uses these technologies and media together to produce an effect that is greater than if consumed alone."[5]

Agencies need to respond to this shift in media consumption by moving with and even ahead of the consumer base. Today, many agency resources continue to pour into traditional media, even as consumers move away from those formats. As consumers spend more time with new media and new technology, so too must agencies and advertising.

To do this, agencies must produce far more interactive advertising. This has to move beyond the original concept of a clickable banner. Interactive advertising has to rise to new levels of creativity, using all the possible interactive options. A clickable banner is still an option, but live chat, blogs, forums, consumer-generated content, and e-mail are other options too. Interactivity invites consumers to be part of the advertising discussion, not simply to receive the finished ad product. It's a process that must evolve and become part of agency dogma. The era of one-way advertising is fading. It's a concept rooted in old media and one ill suited to the way consumers use technology today. Empowered consumers are used to being able to customize their experiences, be it choosing the time and place to receive content or deciding when and how to view an ad. Agencies must create advertising that lives in that mind-set—one in which consumers drive the experience.

Ultimately, to serve these empowered consumers, agencies will need to see their work as device neutral. Rather than create a 30-second TV spot, an ad jingle, or a classified ad, agencies will be called upon to craft advertising that lives on whatever device consumers have handy. The nature of ads will be driven by their core element—text, audio, or video—and it will deliver when and where the consumers demand. Reaching this level of flexibility is a huge challenge to the agency community, which has spent years working in media-specific silos. But as consumers move into their new digital reality, they leave behind the old lines that divided television from print from radio. As they function in a converged experience, advertising will need to be there as well. Agencies will need to create work that delivers messages in a converged world.

SERVE THE CLIENT

The interactive world is one in which the numbers are turned around and long-held truths about consumer behavior crumble. The vacuum left by this shift in media consumption needs to be filled by analytics, and agencies need to help clients connect with this information. It can come from inside the walls of the company, as Publicis Groupe has done by adding analysis expertise in the form of its Denuo division headed by Rishad Tobaccowala. Or it can come from an independent outside firm. But advertisers want their ad partners to help them navigate this world, and navigation requires more than good ideas; it needs metrics.

To serve advertisers, agencies will need to do a better job of serving detailed and actionable analytics. Complex analytics have been available for years to other aspects of industry, such as supply chain and manufacturing. But the marketing industry is only just catching up and beginning to apply this science to its need for accountability. Indeed, a survey fielded by Forrester Research, the Association of National Advertisers, and Marketing Management Analytics found that many are still grappling with their ability to implement and learn from real-time decision tools.[6]

Advertisers need their agencies to overcome concerns and bring more of these tools to the table. Analytics are especially crucial to the successful use of emerging media formats such as blogs. Already, we can measure a blog's success and authority by how many other sites offer links to it. But other measurements are possible. Are we tracking which blogs start conversations? Can we sort them by the demographics of their authors and their visitors? Can they be organized so that advertisers can tap their reach? With the proper metrics, the answer is yes. But advertisers don't have that expertise in house. That's a road map they'll look to their agencies to provide.

Numbers are needed to help big companies make the big decisions to make big changes. A theory will go only so far.

SHIFT THE PARADIGMS

None of these tactical changes will happen unless ad agencies undertake the harder and more ethereal work of a paradigm shift. More than just a change in behavior, shifting the paradigms of the industry means rethinking goals, processes, and underlying assumptions. These are the driving forces of the industry, and digital change puts them up for review.

Shift: Interruption to Invitation

Under traditional media rules, an ad was, by nature, an interruption. It was a break in the use of content, be it television, radio, or print. Agencies were charged with making this the most effective interruption possible. That required skills in timing, knowing when and how to interrupt consumers for the best possible results. It required a degree of finesse and strategy. It also involved following interruption guidelines set out by the media companies. These parameters indicated when and where interruptions were permissible. Advertising, by contract, stayed within those lines.

But as digital convergence sweeps through the industry, the notion of interruptions is being replaced by the new concept of invitation. Rather than break into a content experience, advertising must now create an appealing come-on. The ad must be alluring and intriguing enough for consumers to voluntarily stop what they are doing and move actively into the ad environment. Creating an effective invitation is not the same process as creating an effective interruption. It requires different skills: the invitation must pay off with a longer satisfying experience. The interruption ad, by contrast, is short and over in a matter of seconds. To develop these skills, agencies must recognize the different underlying themes and create ads that work not only with new technical tools but also with new ways of thinking about advertising.

Shift: Demographics to Intentions

The concept of targeting is not new to advertising. For decades, smart agencies have looked to demographics to help them understand how best to position a product and ad campaign. Ads were developed by understanding the demographic hallmarks of the target market. Was the product aimed at baby boomers? Ads featuring rock 'n' roll music fit the bill. Was it aimed at Hispanics? Spots in Spanish, featuring culturally relevant images such as family time, were called for. Was it aimed at young men? Bring on the pretty girls.

But while demographic targeting has produced many success stories, it is a system that is being overtaken by a new set of road rules. Search technology allows advertisers to get closer to the state of one-to-one marketing by creating advertising moments based not on demographics but on intentions. If consumers have indicated by previous search experiences that they are interested in buying a car, advertising can be delivered to those individuals based on intentions, regardless of age or social status. Much can be learned from search history. By the searches and sites clicked, individuals can reveal not just age and economic status but also cultural background, family status, political leanings, and worldview. Advanced search algorithms allow advertisers to understand consumers more deeply than ever before. Demographics got them close; search gets them closer.

This turns agency work on its head. Campaigns that could be designed for 40 million people at a time must now be configured for one-to-one delivery. They must be customizable, flexible, and usable in a search platform, where customer intentions are the driving force.

Shift: One-Way to Two-Way

In its clarion call to the global marketplace, the Cluetrain Manifesto declared "All markets are conversations." This is a significant shift in mind-set for ad agencies, which have lived most of their industrial lives speaking to an audience that rarely talked back.

Agencies have long produced work into a feedback vacuum. Ads went out into the consumer marketplace, and it could be months or years before the vetting of reaction and sales results evaluated the ads' success. But today's marketplace embraces a paradigm shift away from outbound marketing into two-way conversations. New technology allows consumers to say what they think of ads and to talk back to their creators in real time. Let's return for a moment to the discussion of Super Bowl ads. In the early '90s, it was considered a revolutionary move to institute speedy polling that allowed the industry to know in a matter of days which were the most popular ads of the sports contest. Today, that turnaround time can be hours or minutes, as consumers happily flock to their PCs during the game itself to rate and rank the ads they've just seen. This real-time feedback is part of the two-way conversation of the ad industry today.

The yay or nay on an ad can come with frightening speed—and accuracy. When Chrysler introduced its series of ads starring vocal star Celine Dion, mainstream ad reviewers said the carmaker had scored a coup. Dion was famous worldwide and had achieved idol status in her recording of the theme song of the hit movie *Titanic*. But in cyberspace, the chatter took on a different tone. Bloggers and individual consumers wondered whether the Dion story wasn't. Wasn't she overexposed? Wasn't that song on the radio a million times a day? Wasn't this rendition already turning up on spoofs and parodies?

And the virtual mood proved accurate. The ads were artfully done and skillfully placed on high-impact television, yet they failed to excite consumers. The ad campaign was short lived. Critics said Chrysler had overspent on star power.[7]

Ad reviews are just one way consumers talk back. They also do it via e-mail and chat. They conduct their own conversations on blogs and forums. They consider their opinions worthwhile and expect—demand—that the marketing community listen and respond forthwith. This takes the notion of the one-way ad and tosses it to the nostalgia pile. There is no lag time in agency life today. Consumers won't settle for a presentation. They want a dialogue. Agencies will need to learn the language to join the conversation.

Ultimately, advertisers want their agencies to succeed in this evolution. The complex new world of digital marketing is one that companies hope will be made more clear by their hired guns—the companies they've long turned to for advice. But reaching consumers in this new age requires more than just a shift in tactics or a computer upgrade. It requires an understanding of the wholesale revolution taking place in the consumer experience. Agencies must change because the end recipients of their creativity have changed. While there will still be a market of lean-back, passive watchers of advertising fare, the emphasis will shift with the generations, and the new power demographics will approach ads in an entirely new way. Agencies must be ready to reach this new consumer community. Advertisers are counting on them.

Eight

Digital Transformation and Vertical Industries

Which industry has been most affected by digital transformation?

Chances are good that your view on this will be shaped primarily by your industry at the moment. From the inside of any business today, it may feel as though digital change has remade much of what passed for standard operating procedure. That's true for many industries across the board. While each industry may face its individual hurdles, many have followed a similar learning curve—the one that draws them from perceiving the digital transformation to becoming transformed themselves.

It is a process with several moving parts.

First, the leading-edge consumers of any one industry branch out into new territory. They begin to demand new products, new services, and, often, new speed and precision from industry technology. Noticing this demand, leading-edge businesses step into the fray and begin to offer niche products. These are the start-ups of the change process.

As the leading-edge consumers are served by the leading-edge companies, mass-market consumers begin to take notice. Mass-market consumers see the new tactics in the hands of these hip, trend-setting leaders, and they begin to want these products and services for themselves. As the mass-market demand grows, the mass-market providers see the light. They too step up and begin offering what was once considered new and different in the mass-market supply chain.

Finally, brining up the rear, are the laggards. These are the consumers who were perfectly happy with things in the old days and the companies who aren't too happy about change either. But the force of change is strong, and eventually, the laggards are drawn along as well, making the full cycle of industry transformation complete.

While the general cycle of change is common among many industries, it is still instructive to see how each one deals with both the common hurdles and the unique challenges. It is especially critical to watch the industries whose spending is most essential to the ad industry. As they experience (or put off) the digital dream learning curve, the overall fortunes of the ad industry will be affected.

AUTOMOTIVE

Following the general cycle of the change process, the auto industry was first introduced to the concept of digital transformation by its consumers. Car buyers had never been especially satisfied with the buying process. It was long perceived by many consumers that the dealer was in control, the manufacturer seemed removed and aloof, and, ultimately, consumers were at a disadvantage. The structure of the auto sales and manufacturing process was one that was unclear to average consumers. It was hard to emerge from shelling out five figures for a new car and wonder whether you had gotten a poor deal. Many could not help but wonder, was there more to the process than they had known?

The Internet, therefore, filled a critical need on the part of consumers. It offered information and lots of it. Consumers were able to research the product and compare features, availability, options, and—the Holy Grail of the average car shopper—prices. Car shoppers had access to reviews, research, data, multiple retailers, and other car buyers. The information infusion had a distinct impact. Consumers who used to start car shopping by recalling TV ads, checking local newspapers, or visiting a showroom now started the process online. By 2005, shoppers were more likely to look for information from a manufacturer or dealer Web site than they were to get advice from friends or family.[1] More than one-third of adults 18–30 now say that the Internet is the single most important source of automotive information, topping all other information sources including newspapers, magazines, television, friends, and Mom and Dad.[2]

The impact on makers and sellers of cars was significant. The consumers who came into dealerships were not the undecided shoppers the industry was used to. These were empowered consumers of the digital age. They arrived armed with knowledge, comparative pricing, and a strong negotiating position. Initially, the industry was dismayed. This would clearly make it harder for all players in the industry food chain to maintain margins.

But then another consumer Internet trend emerged. In 2005, Jupiter Research released this nugget regarding the behavior of car shoppers online. Most of the online shoppers were not yet sure what car they wanted or where they wanted to buy it, making them prime targets for automotive advertising.[3] This realization helped shift the industry from fear and loathing into digital advertising. Consumers had not really circumvented the sales and marketing process. They had simply started it in a new spot. In the digital age, the Internet was the first platform of the sales cycle.

Auto companies have responded to this shift by beefing up their presence online. Some look to align themselves with the latest in entertainment in hopes that the image will rub off on the brand and prime the online shopper for a test drive. Ford Motor Company, for example, launched a site dedicated to Lincoln Mercury that featured music, chat rooms, and entertainment news. The design and content of the site were aimed at the urban customer looking to Lincoln as the top luxury brand. Other companies were less concerned about entertainment and focused more on getting information out to as many Internet visitors as possible. Toyota's Web site is available in multiple languages, including Spanish and Chinese.

Some auto companies are going a step further, pushing beyond a Web presence into other forms of digital marketing. Mazda ran an e-mail campaign that tapped consumers who had indicated interest in the brand and came away with a 3% conversion rate.[4] An Acura dealership in Illinois installed the latest in live chat technology on its Web site. Visitors to the Web site were greeted by a virtual sales rep—a live person, not an automated sales bot—and offered help.[5]

All this boosted auto's ad buy on the Internet. TNS-MI reporting shows that auto companies spent $147.3 million on Internet advertising in 2001. By 2005, that number had reached $424.1 million.[6]

Does this mean that auto will abandon its old advertising formats? Not likely. While the Internet expertly serves those ready to car shop, it does not do the critical place holding necessary to high-end products such as automobiles. A car is the second biggest purchase most people will make, after a home. It is not purchased often or with speed or whimsy. So it is crucial to be in the consumer's general consciousness so that when car buying time comes along, the brand is top of mind. For that, the industry needs the less targeted, more diffuse, more omnipresent power of television and other traditional media. While the Internet provides the marketing power to attract consumers who have begun searching, other media such as television and magazines provide the brand imagery to whisper in the ear of consumers long before the sales cycle begins. This early influencing is still critical to brand positioning in the auto industry. Even the allure of Internet ads will not take auto advertising from its traditional platforms. The two media—old and new—will share the budget to serve the customers.

MOVIES

One can forgive the movie industry for not immediately recognizing the advertising power of digital transformation. At first blush, the new technology looked more like a threat than an opportunity. The advent of the Internet brought Hollywood a host of new and serious challenges.

First off, digital media were direct competitors to traditional cinema. Eyeballs that would have once gone to a big screen were now distracted by the many new offerings of digital entertainment. Online entertainment in the form of games, videos, social forums, and other content drew dollars, time, and attention away from "old" formats. The precious attention of busy consumers was distracted by this new platform.

Further, the Internet proved a prime platform for pirates. Now, not only could movies be sold on street corners, but also they could be stolen and hawked online to millions around the world. The new technology was a new battleground for copyright protection.

Finally, the digital transformation upended Hollywood's carefully constructed promotion cycle. Studios once planned the advertising and roll out of a feature film with clockwork precision, choosing the day, time, and media format in which to release news and advertising. A precise schedule was set long in advance of opening weekend, with ad buys, publicity, media leaks, and even ticket sales tightly controlled. However, the Internet undermined the movie machinery. Now, long before a studio was ready to market its movie, the fans would already be privy to news and information about it. The Internet allowed hoards of devoted movie fans to do their own sleuthing—and post the purloined news and information online. Movies in production could no longer count on a tight lid. All information, from casting news to location woes to early versions of scripts, turned up on the Internet. Casting changes were made public and twist endings revealed. Nothing was sacred. The media spawned a new cast of commentators, such as Harry Knowles of AintItCool.com, a hero of the movie fan world for his ability to find and distribute movie news. He was lauded by fans but was a thorn in the side of the command and control movie industry.

Still, whatever the industry's reservations about the new media, moviegoers forced the issue of online movie marketing by going online themselves and demanding that Hollywood serve them there.

While moviemakers maintained a traditional marketing mix, their consumers were getting more nontraditional by the day. The Center for the Digital Future reported that by 2005, more than three-quarters of Americans were using the Internet. Nearly two-thirds have it at home. About half have high-speed access. And that's the figure for the total population. Filtered by demographic group, it changes markedly. The rate for high-speed access among college students, for example, reaches 95%.[7]

Not only were consumers already online, but also they were already showing willingness to respond to movie advertising there. A study by ComScore looked at online surfers looking for movie-related content. Among those who just surfed, 20% bought tickets. Among those who saw an ad for a movie during their surfing, 28.2% bought tickets.[8] And consumers were looking for more. Almost half of the consumers in an Outsell poll listed online sources such as Google or the online sites of newspapers as their number one or two choice for entertainment information.[9]

So the movie industry, like other industries, followed its customers online. The motion picture industry spent $44.7 million on Internet display advertising in 2001. By 2005, that budget was up to $71.7 million.[10] What was once considered experimental quickly became standard operating procedure. No movie release is complete without a dedicated Web site. Some films such as *The Blair Witch Project* have achieved fame and financial success backed by online marketing campaigns. New releases often tap the latest in new technology. The Jack Black comedy *Nacho Libre* was marketed in part via podcasts that Black recorded during the filming. Internet journalists such as Harry Knowles were added to regular press lists, and virtual journalists became part of the mainstream conversation. When news of problems on the set of *Scooby-Doo 2* appeared on Internet fan sites, Warner Brothers invited a select group of Internet journalists to the set to observe the changes and improvements to the film in progress.[11]

The movies are still an overwhelmingly traditional media player. While display ad spending online is up overall in the past five years, the rise has not been steady. From 2004 to 2005, spending actually dipped 16.4%.[12] Still, the industry has recognized the power of the new media to influence its customer base. It is making a play to keep the customers who have gone online from leaving the theater altogether.

FINANCIAL SERVICES

The financial services industry owes a lot to the digital transformation. It was the Internet boom and the stock frenzy that followed that made so many ordinary Americans into finance fans. While previously, many consumers were content to stick their savings into whatever the bank was selling, the advent of the Internet boom made millions into stock pickers. Money management became a national pastime. The financial services industry boomed right along with the Internet economy. New companies, new products, and new services all sprang up to serve these newly empowered financial consumers.

The bubble burst, but financial services remained devoted to the medium that helped it expand. It was one of the industries quickest to see the value in online advertising, rising from $869.7 million in online display ad spending in 2001 to more than $1 billion in 2005.[13] Financial services companies realized that consumers, once used to researching and managing their money online, were not going to give back the tools and return to the old days. Empowered consumers had arrived for this industry as well.

Financial services has met its digital future primarily on two fronts: branding and promotions. The surge in coverage of financial services in the Internet news media has opened a spate of platforms for banner and other clickable ads. Also, behavioral targeting is particularly suited to this industry. Consumers who show their intentions to find out about a particular investment vehicle are clearly ripe for an ad in this subject area. Companies are also able to drive click-throughs via e-mail marketing.

On branding, experts say financial services still struggles to harness the power of the digital platform. Companies have wrestled with the difficulty of taking rich traditional media campaigns and making them work in the Internet space. A report from Forrester Research shows that often the telling details and evocative imagery are lost in the translation. Take, for example, the advertising by Vanguard. In the glossy magazine spread, the design recalls a children's storybook, with fairy-tale fonts and hand-drawn illustrations. When moving the same ad online, the visuals are lost. "If prospects get interested by the ads and go to the site, they'll see none of these visual elements—and may even wonder if they came to the right place," writes Forrester analyst Harley Manning, author of *Making the Most of Your Financial Services Brand on the Web*.[14]

Indeed, most of the companies surveyed by Forrester flunked the overall branding exercise. Too often, the stated desire to be customer centric was met with a Web site that neglected the fundamentals of good customer experience or didn't keep up with the company's traditional media ad campaigns.[15]

But the industry is in the digital world to stay. Consumer interest in personal finance continues to soar. As boomers head for retirement, they'll be even more eager to understand and manage their investments and financial prospects. As a younger generation reaches investment age, it will turn to the information source it has used to make sense of life all along—the Internet. At the same time, newspapers, once the regular source of market information, are cutting back on traditional information services, such as stock agate and other tables. Indeed, *The New York Times* has moved to cut its stock tables. That will only drive more consumers to the Web for content, branded and otherwise.

CONSUMER PRODUCTS

Consumer packaged goods (CPG) companies have been eager to embrace the Internet. The digital world gives them a platform to reach millions, and the economics are substantially cheaper. It was consumer products giant Procter & Gamble (P&G) that sounded the ad industry clarion call in 1994 when then P&G CEO Ed Artzt berated the advertising industry for not being better versed in the art of advertising online. The CPG giant knew it would be the milieu of the new millennium. His call to action still resonates today:

> "Now, we're going to have to grab technology in our teeth again and make it work for us. But it isn't going to be as simple as it was to adapt to radio or TV, where everything favored the advertiser. Now, we've got competition, not just among traditional, ad-supported media but from unadvertised programming as well—entertainment and information that will represent an entirely separate source of revenue for media suppliers and programmers alike. This is a real threat. These new media suppliers will give consumers what they want and potentially at a price they're willing to pay. If user fees replace advertising revenue, we're in serious trouble."[16]

The industry responded, but the road to digital success has been bumpy.

Take Kraft. After paying to have its ads distributed through the Google network, the company was horrified last year to see its logo turn up on the site of a white supremacist organization. It happened because the white supremacist site improperly copied code to place the search engine on its own site. But the experience was a wake-up call for brands: the Web is not always a secure ad environment.[17]

Coupons, too, proved a challenge. At first blush, many in the industry figured the Internet would make a cheap and easy new way to target and distribute coupons. However, early efforts have not proved smooth. Fraud became a huge problem in the early efforts. Manufacturers found it difficult to issue their own online coupons and keep tabs on fraudulent coupon efforts. Also, manufacturers found they also had legitimate competition for coupon users online. Retailers were using their Web sites to issue their own virtual coupons, thus creating additional challenges for the manufacturer. Finally, online coupons remain a difficult marketing program to measure. With all these challenges, the progress toward online couponing has been slow. Certainly it has grown, but it is not anywhere near the boom business everyone predicted back in the early '90s.

Still, the potential to acquire new customers at pennies per pop keeps the industry coming back for more digital options.

Integrated campaigns are taking much of the glory in the CPG world. The ad campaign for Dove's new line of Calming Night soaps and lotions relied on the marriage of old and new media. Television spots, featuring stars such as *Desperate Housewives'* Felicity Huffman, drove women to the dedicated mini-site DoveNight.com. On the site were three specially crafted Webisodes starring Huffman and developed by Penny Marshall.

The industry is also starting to leverage technology in stores. Grocers are using kiosks to deliver coupons, promotions, and even individualized offers of discounts and specials. In-store networks and digital signage are being leveraged to improve and speed customer service. Cell phone users say they would be interested in receiving offers of discounts and specials during shopping trips. Bringing the in-store experience into the digital age will be key to the survival of the grocery store, writes Forrester analyst Tamara Mendelsohn:

> "Consumers want promotions and discounts on products that they are interested in. Grocers that allow consumers to build shopping lists at home via the Web and then access them in the store can save consumers time by highlighting where the products on their list are located in the store and remind them of previously purchased products they might want to buy. Grocers can use the shopping list information to offer targeted promotions on items in the list when it's printed out in the store, ensuring that offers are both relevant and timely."[18]

Overall, Internet display ad spending in the packaged goods industry has grown from $106 million in 2001 to $267.4 million in 2005.[19] While some tactics such as coupons and site ads remain a challenge, others such as branded Web sites are helping brands to make new connections to consumers in their emerging digital reality. Industry leadership has been unwilling to let the new technology sever the advertising bond between manufacturer and consumer. Said Artzt at the close of his speech to the American Association of Advertising Agencies:

> "We can use interactive technology to engage consumers in our commercials. We can provide direct response. If a consumer wants to know which Cover Girl nail polish matches the lipstick she saw in our commercial, we can tell her on the spot. We can target not just demographic segments, but individual households. If a family has a newborn baby, we can make sure they get a Pampers commercial. We can use games, infomercials, video shopping malls. We'll have a whole bag of tools to engage and inform consumers, and if we do that right, we can keep people in their seats when the commercials come on. History says the advertising industry adapts brilliantly to new technology. But we can't just sit there. We have to act."[20]

PHARMACEUTICALS

The pharmaceutical industry had a slightly different path to digital advertising. It was not an industry free to follow its consumers to the Internet. Indeed, until 1997, it was not free to follow its consumers at all. Direct-to-consumer advertising was allowed only after the Food and Drug Administration changed its guidelines, and even then, the industry is tightly regulated and scrutinized. Every attempt to reach out to average consumers, in any media, new or old, is up for constant and consistent review. The final rules are not yet written for pharmaceutical advertising. It is an advertising category in flux.

This has not kept it offline. Online display ad spending for the category has had a spectacular rise. It has grown from $18.8 million in

2001 to $155.4 million in 2005.[21] The biggest single-year jump came between 2003 and 2004, when spending zoomed 205.3%. Although the business cooled some in the following year, with dollar spending falling 12%, the overall investment in the digital transformation is still significant.[22] As an industry, pharmaceuticals has embraced the digital future.

As was the case in auto and personal finance, the impetus came in part from the end users of the product. Consumers came online demanding more information about health care. After generations of doctor-patient relationships in which only one party had access to health care knowledge, now the Internet had made educated consumers out of the traditional patients. Health care consumers sought out details on doctors, hospitals, illnesses, and, of course, treatments. Pharmaceutical firms stepped up with Web sites, e-mail campaigns, and other online content designed to give health care consumers what they were surfing for: information.

Direct-to-consumer advertising had a big impact on the doctor-patient relationship. Doctors began reporting that patients were turning up in examination rooms and asking for medications by brand name. Doctors also had to cope with the free flow of information among consumers. Forums, blogs, and e-mail conversations allowed patients to better understand conditions and possible treatments.

Pharmaceutical companies have plunged with determination into this empowered health care consumer zone. In many ways, their advertising recruits consumers to act as the final ambassadors to the doctor's office. Drug ad sites offered information, wellness tools, personal stories, and even coupons—everything but a prescription pad.

Recruiting new consumers is not the only way pharmaceutical companies have learned to use the digital platform. Many also have marshaled digital tools as public relations tactics. Pharmaceutical company Web sites, in addition to consumer information, often sport background and position papers outlining the charitable works of the company or the role long-term research plays in the fight against disease. For an industry constantly having to explain why its tiny little pills are so expensive, the Internet offers a spokesperson who is always on.

The pharmaceutical industry's place in digital advertising is not set in stone. Concerns over how direct-to-consumer advertising affects patient health and health care costs may ultimately limit the practice. The regulators who freed the drug companies to advertising may come to demand that some of that freedom be curtailed. Already, lawmakers are revisiting guidelines with an eye toward making adjustments and shifts to maintain the flow of information while protecting the public from a health care hard sell. But as Forrester analyst Bradford J. Holmes writes in his report "Consumer Marketing in Health Care," the genie is out of the medicine bottle.

> "The FDA tightly controls all Rx and device marketing and HIPAA constrains the personalization of communications from plans and providers to and among consumers. But that is not going to stop consumers from blogging about their plans, their aches and preferred cures, updating wikis about stains or otherwise shaping their own views on the stuff that companies have to sell."[23]

Health care marketers, he says, will need to stay in the digital conversation or have it go on without them.

All of these industries have their own particular stories, their own challenges, their own hurdles to overcome. Yet, they have much in common. They have wrestled with new technology and watched it as it rose to prominence and began to impact the processes and procedures they had worked years to establish. They have all come to face the reality of digital transformation and the new business tools and challenges it presents.

Nine

Law and Order

Change often precedes society's ability to manage it. That is true in social experience. It is true in politics. It is certainly true today at the junction of technology and commerce. Change has swept these industries with such speed, in many cases, that it has outpaced the boundaries of law and regulation.

In the middle ground of change in progress, legal constructs and existing agencies are often at a loss to offer guidance. Attempts to stretch existing regulations to meet the shifting needs often fall short. Few are happy with the results. Regulators fret at the limits of their abilities. Change agents chafe at the restrictions. It is the moment at which society's grid of rules and regulations must rise and morph to meet the new demands of the day.

We are now in that middle swath of a changing but not fully changed landscape. Much is new. Much more newness is to come in the near term. Around this shifting experience, lawmakers, theorists, advocates, and business leaders have begun the conversation about how this change will be managed. In the coming years, law will begin to evolve out of early cases.

What will be the nature of this new law and order? It will take shape in the coming years. But some early topics have emerged, sure to be the first recipients of the developing digital legal landscape.

BEHAVIORAL TARGETING

"How may I help you?"

A hallmark of just how drastic the change in our society has been is tied up in that common little phrase. In the traditional setting of the brick-and-mortar store, this phrase is welcome. It is the mark of customer service. It demonstrates the intention of the merchant to approach the customer, find out what he or she needs, and set about making that person happy. In a store, the phrase is welcome.

On the Internet, it's the beginning of a legal debate.

Digital convergence has brought with it a host of complications, but one of the knottiest is the tangled conversation around the art of customer service online. At the core of the issue is a disagreement over just how closely an individual can be monitored before the attentive merchant morphs into Big Brother. At what point is technological innovation an invasion of privacy?

Marketers, of course, want to tap every means available to reach into the inner minds of consumers. They live to give customers what they want, and the more accurately they can perceive those wants, the more quickly and successfully they can meet those desires with products and services. Marketers have been trying to crawl inside the heads of consumers for generations. Tactics such as the focus group, the telephone poll, even the suggestion box, have emerged, all as marketers strive to learn what it is that customers really want.

That being the case, the advent of customer-tracking technology ranks as one of the great moments in marketing history. Now tools have emerged that help marketers know the truth. They can watch and track as visitors surf a Web site. They can measure and analyze the patterns. And, with the advent of search technology, marketers can hope to gather a full array of consumer behavior and slice and dice it carefully to construct a clear picture of the hopes and desires of their target market. Cashing in on that information with the right message at the right time is what the industry has dubbed "behavioral targeting." It is the science of analyzing how consumers behave online and using that information as a map for ad messages. Consumers who tap an Internet search engine with the keyword "MP3" will get an ad for the latest iPod—and its competitors. Typing "mortgage rates" into the search field results in ads for brokers, home builders, maybe even a furniture store. Marketers are finding ways to do what they have long wished was possible: read consumers' minds and react with the perfect product.

Digital dreamers have already begun planning the next incarnation of marketer mind reading. Behavioral targeting is a process that can be stretched far beyond any one search session. In the near future, when consumers will toggle all day between desktop, handheld, and networked devices, behavioral targeting will be leveraged to bring advertising to consumers any place, any time. A consumer who searches for sports cars one morning on a desktop will find related ads delivered to his laptop later in the day. A fashionista using her cell phone Internet search capability to find the hot local shoe store may receive banner ads featuring the latest in footwear on her office computer a day later. Time and place, long the confines of advertising, will lose their meaning, and all advertising will focus on the previous behaviors of the consumers. What consumers want is what consumers will get.

But what looks to marketers as advertising nirvana rubs some consumer advocates the wrong way, and they are looking to the legal system for remedy. The concept that marketers are tracking and analyzing a consumer's every move is just a little bit creepy. At what point, they say, does customer behavior analysis become the virtual equivalent of tailing a shopper through the aisles of a store—and then following the consumer home? How much can a marketer glean from amassing a dossier on any one person's search behavior? And how happy would an individual be to share those inner desires? Finally, isn't the ability to track and respond to search patterns simply the used car salesperson come to the Internet? The pushy huckster who just won't leave you alone? That is not progress, they say. That is a consumer nightmare: a world in which the marketer knows everything about you and is using it to sell you something.

Beyond the reactions of average consumers, privacy advocates worry about what will happen when business begins to make a market in consumer data. It is one thing for consumers to know that a favorite retailer or marketer is tracking their activities. But what does it mean for those consumers when the information is bought and sold to any number of commercial interests? Is that then too much information out in the atmosphere? Have consumers been made to give up too much control?

The debate has developed to be one between the technorati and the privacy advocates. Those who originally amassed to fend off the Internet's first threat—identity theft—have now latched on to the issue of behavioral targeting and are framing it as a privacy issue. How much should marketers know about you? How much do you want to share? How comfortable are you with the concept of software tracking your behavior and delivering ads to you as a result? Consumers, advocates argue, should have control over their data and not have it mined by companies without their knowledge.

The pro-technology camp responds: all targeting is good. Any time a marketer can better understand consumers and deliver more accurate, relevant messages, everyone wins. Consumers have a more satisfying experience, and the marketer makes a sale.

What do consumers say? They are only just beginning to weigh in. While the professionals battle it out over behavioral targeting, consumers are not yet the loudest voices in the debate. This is ironic because each side claims to have the best interests of the consumers at heart. But consumers have not yet expressed clearly where their hearts lie.

Indeed, when it comes to behavioral targeting, consumers are open but not wedded to the concept. They are interested in the notion of a tailored marketing experience—one in which ads are never boring, never a waste of time, never irrelevant. Still, they are wise enough to know that not all online promises pan out. They are open to seeing what the experience is like but not yet committed to making it a full-out life change until some results can be felt. It is an agreement to date but not yet marry—though that possibility is on the table if the marketing community delivers a positive experience.

Still, consumers have begun to tell us what they do not like about the practice of targeting. A study by the Pew Internet and American Life Project revealed that consumers are beginning to understand spyware and how it is affecting not only their sense of privacy but also their hardware. Says report author Susannah Fox:

> "91% of internet users have changed their online behavior for fear of becoming victims. Computer programs that secretly plant themselves on people's computers and then monitor users' online behavior or hijack their browsers have become a scourge."[1]

Consumers have begun, Fox says, to change their behavior to avoid spyware:

> "These survey results show that as internet users gain experience with spyware and adware, they are more likely to say they are changing their behavior. But what is more alarming is the larger universe of people who have struggled with mysterious computer problems, but have no idea why. Internet users are increasingly frustrated and frightened that they are not in charge of their internet experience."[2]

The debate has moved beyond the theoretical and onto the radar screen of America's lawmakers. Among their efforts:

- Senator Diane Feinstein (D-CA) introduced privacy legislation that would regulate the collection and use of personally identifiable information. Marketers would be required to provide consumers with notice and an opt-out option.
- Senator Charles Schumer (D-NY) introduced legislation that would create an Office of Identity Theft in the Federal Trade

Commission. That office would regulate how consumer information is collected, maintained, and sold.

- Senator Bill Nelson (D-FL) introduced the Information Protection and Security Act, which would charge the Federal Trade Commission (FTC) with regulating information brokers. A companion bill was introduced in the House of Representatives.

There are many more examples, and they follow a similar pattern: elected officials are moving to put their stamp on the progress of digital consumer information. Advertising groups have reacted with alarm to the growing legislative drum beat. Says the Association of National Advertisers (ANA):

"ANA believes the free flow of and access to consumer information provides substantial benefits to the economy. We recognize, however, a need to ensure the safety and security of personal information. ANA has supported various efforts, both private and public, to protect consumer privacy. We were an early supporter of private sector initiatives, including self-regulatory best practices programs and seal programs. The FTC is also very active in enforcing privacy laws already on the books. These initiatives strike the best balance between consumer concerns and the viability of consumer marketing. We oppose broad privacy legislation that would impose an 'opt-in' regime, as this would severely limit the information available to marketers, would hurt economic efficiency and thereby adversely affect consumers."[3]

Eric Goldman, assistant professor at Santa Clara University School of Law, argues that casting a negative spin over the act of data mining is distracting lawmakers and business experts from the real work at hand.

"In this respect, data mining concerns are analogous to concerns about the regulation of new technologies. The technology community regularly argues that regulators should outlaw bad technology uses, not the technology itself. I advocate a similar approach to data mining. Data mining is not the problem; the problem is the bad uses of mined data, and that is where our focus should be."[4]

Going forward, marketers will need to proceed with the evolution into behavioral targeting with both caution and clarity of purpose. It will be crucial to see the early efforts run their full course so that lessons can be learned and patterns can be noted. But even as these experiments move ahead, marketers must keep a close watch on consumer mood. The most important ingredient to the success of behavioral targeting is not technology or even supportive regulation; it is consumer buy-in. If consumers are behind the process—because they can see the benefits in their daily lives—then it will emerge as a new standard in marketing practice. If consumers turn on the practice thanks to negative experiences, it can end up a footnote, filed under great ideas that never took hold.

CLICK FRAUD

While lawmakers debate the theoretical pros and cons of technology, some businesses are dealing with far more concrete woes. One of the most vexing legal problems of the emerging online ad world is the threat of click fraud. In its early days, click fraud was a petty ante crime. Amateur affiliate marketers were often accused of clicking on each other's ads to drive up traffic counts. But what was once a minor annoyance has emerged as a crime drama. Online advertising has boomed, and the stakes are now higher. In 2006, Yahoo! entered into a click fraud settlement that would pay $5 million to advertisers. Google said it would pay $90 million in advertising credits and attorney's fees to settle a class action suit over click fraud.[5]

Search engine leaders say click fraud is overestimated. Often, they say, what looks like fraud is actually a quirk of large Internet Service Providers (ISPs) in operation.

But the topic is not going away. Latest estimates posit that click fraud represents a $1.3-billion-a-year advertising revenue loss—this includes $800 million wasted on fraudulent clicks plus $500 million held back from pay-per-click (PPC) advertising spending.[6] A 2006 study by Outsell found that among 400 advertisers responsible for approximately $1 billion in ad spending, respondents estimated that 14.6% of the clicks they are billed for are not actual consumers responding to the ad.[7]

Concerns over click fraud have direct impact on the growth of the online ad industry, the report states. Already, 27% of advertisers have slowed PPC ad buying, including 16% of that group that has stopped PPC spending completely. Another 10% of current advertisers acknowledged plans to cut PPC spending in the future.[8]

Click fraud can take a variety of forms. In many cases, it is the work of a rival, hoping to undermine a competitor's ad efforts. Companies may seek to hurt a competitor by constantly clicking on the opposition's ads—thereby running up the bill without providing any hope of payoff. This kind of corporate warfare can be carried out by software programs, making it easy and often quite damaging to the target. There are other forms, such as bots that are programmed to roam the Web and click on links associated with advertisers and search engine marketing firms that trade in inflated click reports to drive up their prices. All have caught the attention of a nervous industry.

Companies that suspect click fraud have been particularly frustrated with their ability to do anything about it. Take the experience of Radiator.com, the Web version of auto radiator wholesaler Radiator Express Warehouse. Radiator.com was spending $20,000 a month for ads on search engines such as Google and Yahoo! At first, the company was pleased with its results and quickly boosted its search engine spending. The experience seemed so positive that company executives said Google wrote up a case study on the company. But when conducting a review of its search engine activity, the company hired an outside auditor and was told that up to 35% of the clicks were actually fraudulent. The company is pursuing legal action to recoup what it says are losses to fraud.[9]

AIT, a Web hosting company in Fayetteville, Arkansas, had a similar problem. The company says it spent $475,000 in advertising with

Google between 2003 and 2005. When the company noticed that its returns on the investment were declining, an audit of click activity turned up evidence of click fraud, said Chief Executive Clarence Briggs. Google failed to provide adequate information and enforcement regarding click fraud, he says. He also has gone to court to settle his dispute. "The real threat here is to the concept of paid search and ultimately to the entire Internet," said Briggs. "If people lose confidence in the commercial viability of the Internet, it threatens the very idea of an emerging global, digital economy. Sooner or later, if something isn't done, the second Internet bubble will burst."[10]

How many clicks are fraudulent? The numbers are all over the board, and there is no clear industry estimate. It is possible that fraud is a small fraction of the total picture. But like news of one shark attack on the Eastern seaboard, the few cases are enough to keep some marketers out of the water. One thing is clear: some level of fraud is taking place. On that information alone, marketers will need to step up and demand attention and changes to the problem. Marketers need to police their own Internet efforts and not merely rely on today's virtual law enforcement to do the job. While that may evolve, today, marketers must be participants in their own Internet security. Understanding the click advertising technicalities is key to making sense of the tactic and its ROI.

Marketers and agencies must also continue to demand that the search engine community come up with products that reduce the opportunity for fraud. Google, for example, is rolling out a system by which marketers pay for a click and an action rather than just a click in order to cut down on the opportunity for fraud.[11]

Also, the industry will need to develop audit standards for this new breed of advertising. Advertisers in other media, such as television, receive audited, notarized reports detailing the delivery of the ads for which they've paid. Search advertisers currently have no such option. Instead, many are contractually obligated to take the search engine's word for it. Clearly, as the debate over click fraud ties up the time and energy of all involved, that standard will have to evolve.

Other legal issues are also brewing, and many involve the wild west landscape of search engine marketing. As technologists and advertisers feel their way toward the future, disputes can and will arise over the outcomes.

PLACEMENT

As technology attorney Eric Goldman noted in his blog, another day, another lawsuit regarding search engine placement. As more consumers make the search process their first stop in a purchase decision, more companies are putting cash into search engine marketing. And nothing frustrates a marketer more than typing the corporate name into a search engine and seeing a rival's site pop up higher in the rankings.

KinderStart, a parenting Web site, took Google to court, alleging that its business took a hit after the search engine giant handed it lower rankings. The company is hardly the only firm suing over search engine placement. SearchKing made a similar legal claim, and California businessman Avi Datner sued Yahoo! because the search engine dropped his site, Partypop.com, from its database.[12] The question over search engine placement is a thorny one and likely to bubble through the courts for some time. Why? Because it is unclear what, if anything, the search engines are required to deliver to marketers when it comes to placement. Search engines argue that they have First Amendment rights and can list search results in any way they please. They further maintain that their criteria for site placement and the software that handles this display are proprietary and they are not required to disclose them.

The issue involves more than just the placement of a company's name in search rankings. Not only are marketers clamoring for placement, but also they are demanding better transparency. For all their faults, old media are known industries. Marketers can make concrete assumptions about their ad spends. Buying time on a particular TV show or placing a classified in a newspaper can be expected to yield certain results—or at least certain contact with consumers. But less is understood about the ways and means of the search engine, and that leaves marketers wondering whether they have made a smart investment. Whether they paid for placement via a search engine's ad program or whether they designed their sites to try to be picked up organically by the software's methodology, they have made an investment in an ad vehicle. Now, they are demanding the auditing and transparency they receive from other media. Thus far, it has been a transparency that search engines have been unwilling to serve up.

Who will get legal status in this dispute? It remains to be seen as the cases work their way through the morass. However, one important element has emerged: marketers will need to come to grips with the concept that search engines are corporate entities, with their own business goals at heart. They are not public spaces to which everyone and anyone may have equal access. Like any other media vehicle, the search engines will consider their own needs first. Techdirt, a Web site devoted to corporate technology issues, posts this comment from its CEO Michael Masnick:

> "From a business owner's perspective, it's your responsibility not to become too dependent on a single supplier. Basing your entire business on your great Google rank is extremely risky—and if your only backup strategy is to sue Google for not ranking you higher, it suggests that your business strategy needs a pretty massive rewrite."[13]

TRADEMARKS

A related issue working its way through legal departments regards the use of trademarks on the Internet and particularly in search engine marketing. This topic so far has been characterized by slow-moving proceedings and contradictory rulings. Consider the case of *JR Cigars v. GoTo.com*. This dispute is six years old. It alleges that cigar seller JR Cigars was harmed when a search engine sold keywords including "JR Cigar," "J R Cigar," "J & R Cigar," "J-R Cigar," "JRCigars.com," and "800 JR Cigar" to various JR competitors. All of the cigar competitors have settled. That leaves JR Cigars pursuing its search engine defendant—first GoTo.com, since bought by Overture, since purchased by Yahoo! And the case drags on.

Other companies are also bogged down in legal disputes over their trademarks in search engine marketing. Geico is one. American Blinds and Wallpaper Factory is another. Thus far, no one case has come to a resolution that provides a guiding principle to the business. Indeed, many rules contradict one another, leaving the only surefire prediction of continued legal wrangling.

While legal action is an expensive and time-consuming process, it is the natural process by which the new rules of this digital advertising game will be constructed. Pioneers of the emerging digital ad formats will run up against new situations and new debates that will require either an agreement or a ruling. The process is not quick. It often requires that business parties educate the legal system as to the new realities of technology and commerce. Still, it is the road the industry must travel toward the new legal framework.

Additionally, lawmakers will need to be brought into the process. In this process, it is critical that marketers participate in the conversation, via advocacy and industry groups. As Washington begins to involve itself in the making of new laws, industry must be prepared to provide information about how the new digital platform runs and what its implications are for the societal good.

The legal challenges of the digital transformation will not be just within our borders. As technology connects the world, purveyors of information will face the hurdles of legal systems around the world. Already, we see companies such as Google wrestling with concepts of free speech in countries such as China. Taking the Western concept of digital transformation into the world market will take us into legal conversations we can only imagine.

But the start of the digital era's new legal framework will begin at home. As we move into the new space of digital transformation, all elements around us will shift. Just as the consumer has changed and the technology we use has changed, so too has the infrastructure of rules and regulations. The legal system is one of the many interested parties that must recognize the digital transformation and make the decision to revamp itself to deal with the new reality. Marketers and agencies, already on the path, must be willing to blaze that trail and offer guidance to the industries that follow.

Ten

The Potential Dark Side

Nothing is all black and white, and digital transformation is no exception. While the shift taking place in technology and commerce offers a great potential upside, there are plenty of ways the change process can go awry. Change left to its own devices often wanders off its best possible course.

In this period of change, it is incumbent upon all industry players to be bold and step up, but at the same time, it is wise to look ahead and recognize the possible pitfalls. As much as we can stay ahead of the missteps, we will create an atmosphere in which digital transformation happens for the greater economic and social good.

The apocryphal Murphy said anything that can go wrong will. A somewhat less dismal but potentially dangerous future lies ahead for the advertising industry. Things can go wrong. The question is, can we get out ahead of the process, or is Murphy right?

The critical move: while embracing and celebrating the possible, keep a weather eye out for the dark side of digital transformation. It is out there—and it demands our attention.

PRIVACY WOES AND CONSUMER BACKLASH

Already, issues over privacy have materialized as a threat to the emergence of digital convergence. Consumers are increasingly worried about who is mining their personal information and what's being done with that data. Certainly, consumers are warm to the idea that data mining can produce better targeted ads and more attractive products and services. But they are wary that not everyone who taps into their information has aboveboard upstanding interests at heart.

Sadly, they are not wrong. Instances of privacy breaches are cropping up with alarming regularity.

In May 2006, the Department of Veterans Affairs (VA) revealed that the personal information of 26 million veterans had been compromised when the home of a VA employee was burglarized and a laptop and external hard drive containing these data were stolen. While the hardware was eventually recovered and experts believe the data were not used by the thieves, the Office of the Inspector General issued a blistering report later that summer that criticized the VA for both its poor data security and its lack of urgency responding to the breach. Most worrisome, wrote Inspector General George J. Opfer, is the lack of procedures and policies in place to prevent further such incidents:

> "We found a patchwork of polices that were difficult to locate and fragmented. None of the policies prohibited the removal of protected information from the worksite or storing protected information on a personally-owned computer, and did not provide safeguards for electronic data stored on portable media or a personal computer."[1]

Further, the report criticized the first response of VA officials when notified of the data breach. Supervisors told Opfer they did not perceive the data breach as a crisis and "failed to recognize the magnitude of the whole thing."[2]

Meanwhile, for several weeks until the matter was resolved, regulators, privacy experts, and hundreds of thousands of consumers worried that their key personal information had been turned over to the dark side.

The "case of the burgled laptop" is just one of the more high-profile cases of data loss to hit the news recently. Wells Fargo faced a lawsuit by consumers who went to court after their personal financial data were stolen from a contractor who had not encrypted the information. The judge ruled that the bank was not liable because the information had not been misused.[3] But consumers will certainly sympathize with the angry bank customers who claimed they lost money, time, and sleep over the incident.

Smaller breaches also cause worry. Western Illinois University revealed that hackers had entered its networks and more than 180,000 students and alumni may have had everything from their credit card numbers to their Social Security numbers stolen. Also at risk: individuals who purchased items from the school's online bookstore.[4]

These examples are just small elements of what has emerged as a primary threat to the success of digital transformation. The ultimate goal of one-to-one marketing rests on a key buy-in from consumers. They must be willing to share their data with marketers and their wants and histories and experiences with commercial interests. It's only through this sharing that the more intense and focused marketing connection can be made. For generations, marketers have been forced to guess at what consumers really want. More recently, they've been able to tap more sophisticated polling and focus group processes. But it is the ability to track a single consumer and mine a single person's data that offers the true leap forward in marketing. No more guessing: consumers can tell us what they want—but only if they feel safe in doing so.

Privacy breaches cut at the very core of digital possibilities. If consumers begin to distrust the system and worry that data are not safe and not secure, then the sharing will end. Consumer backlash will set in, and data will be safeguarded with all possible tools. One-to-one marketing will wither and die.

Keep in mind that it is not just illegal data mining that has consumers worried. Indeed, even data mining that is perfectly legal by current regulatory standards is raising some hackles. Take spam. Consumers reacted with annoyance and chagrin as they found their e-mail addresses co-opted without their permission for commercial purposes. Spam quickly became the prime example of Internet marketers run amok. A sense that marketers were overstepping their bounds, invading the personal space of consumers without permission, resulted in backlash. Filters designed to block e-mail marketing sprang up. Even marketers with permission found themselves sucked into the vortex.

Other examples: adware and spyware. Average computer users, frustrated by the number of times their screens freeze and their systems crash, are beginning to understand that it's not the machines at fault.

A study by the Pew Internet and American Life Project finds that many people are now realizing that the sources of their sluggish computing are adware and spyware. This is just another way consumers are experiencing the digital invasion of privacy. While this may seem more benign—no one is stealing identities or liquidating bank accounts—consumers still perceive adware and spyware as privacy threats. They are intrusions by commercial interests, infiltrating their personal computers. The emphasis is on the word "personal": consumers believe they are alone with their screens, not logged into a massive global focus group. As they realize that companies are sending secret surveyors to their technology, tapping into their experiences without permission, the sense of privacy invasion is strong.[5] Susannah Fox, associate director of the Pew Internet and American Life Project wrote:

> "The threat of unwanted software programs is making people more cautious online. Most internet users think symptoms of spyware are serious problems rather than simply minor annoyances. Millions of internet users have first-hand experience with computer problems related to software intrusions and while many express confidence

and knowledge of the issues, most think more should be done to guard against spyware and notify people about adware."[6]

Consumers are already reacting to the adware and spyware experience by avoiding sites they think aid and abet the practice. That is already a threat to the hopes of digital advertising. Any time consumers pull back from the sharing of data, marketers are left with less to mine and less information with which to make decisions.

Worries over privacy are a primary threat to the success of the digital transformation. If consumers do not trust the process, they will not participate. The advertising industry must address privacy issues in all their forms. They will extend from the obvious and criminal acts of identity theft to more ordinary and everyday actions such as e-mailing without permission. While the industry may make a distinction, consumers may be similarly distressed: a corporate interest is using their personal information without their permission. That reaction can occur whether the item is a Social Security number, an e-mail address, or an Internet surfing pattern. If consumers have the feeling that someone is watching—and making a buck—without their knowledge, the bond of trust between marketer and consumer is broken.

Without trust, consumers will naturally pull back from the one-to-one experience. Targeted marketing is nice, but it's not worth the risk if consumers worry that their data and their interests are on the line.

RESISTANCE AND FISSURE

As with any substantial societal change, digital transformation will take place across several key industries. Marketers, agencies, media, and metrics firms will need to work in concert by stepping up to the idea of change and moving forward with new ideas and new constructs to satisfy the shifting marketplace. In the best-case scenario, all of these industries come together in a centralized decision to move ahead. On the other side of that coin is the pitfall: resistance.

Resistance, said a *Star Trek* villain, is futile. In the case of digital transformation, resistance is actually a threat. Resistance to the changes sweeping consumers and their expectations undermines the advertising industry's ability to succeed. It takes only one element of the overall marketing experience to resist change, and the ripple effect hits us all.

For example, suppose that advertising agencies, as an industry group, opt to maintain focus on traditional media and put their creativity, resources, and planning into elements with long and distinguished histories. Suppose further that this industry segment rejected the notion of digital transformation and viewed it as a fad or perhaps a financially negligible niche in the ad world.

The initial impact would be in the agencies themselves as a loss of revenues and reputation. But the impact would then widen. Agencies would be less able to serve clients, who would have looked to their longtime advisors for guidance. Clients would miss opportunities to connect with consumers. Ultimately, this leads to a fissure in the agency-client relationship. For decades, major marketers have relied upon their agencies to understand the currents of the advertising world. They look to their creative and media buying experts for the detailed knowledge of change in progress. If the agency community were to resist change, clients would need to look elsewhere, and a long-standing partnership between two industries, marketers and agencies, would falter. A fissure leaves clients without advice and agencies without clients.

These splits are already cropping up. Marketers looking for creative expertise in video on demand have found that their traditional shops are not staffed in the niche and have had to look outside for help. "Creative people need to be engaged in the whole process," said Mitch Oscar, executive vice president at Carat Digital.[7] Without creative ad talent focused on the cutting-edge options, marketers are left without key tools and guidance.

Resistance in other quadrants of the industry would be equally problematic. If traditional media fail to embrace change and look for new media incarnations of information, the result is again a split. Embracing change can mean everything from offering digital versions of traditional media to remaking traditional rules of ad sales. When media fail to update themselves, marketers take the initiative. In 2006, Johnson & Johnson opted to sit out the traditional upfront buying season and held out its $400 million in ad money for new and more creative advertising deals. "As a marketer, Johnson & Johnson is looking for new possibilities," said Brian Perkins, J&J's corporate vice president. "That includes being open to the ideas of new advertising agencies."[8]

By resisting change, media brands long considered key conduits to consumers will be displaced. The same is true for the producers of goods and services. Marketers insisting on old-line advertising formats when new ones are emerging set themselves up for disappointment. The metrics industry must also shift with the times or be left behind. Marketers, agencies, and media depend upon the accurate measurement of the viewing audience, both in traditional media and now in the new formats brought about by digital transformation. Resistance to the change leaves the industry players without a road map to the future.

The essence of success in the digital future rests on these intertwined, interdependent industries moving forward in concert. Each relies on the investment of energy and initiative from the others. If one segment resists, one industry holds back, and the rest are affected. The success of all is threatened.

PIRACY

How much are content producers losing to online piracy? The estimates vary widely. But there is agreement on one front: it is a growing problem and one that is only fueled as the digital transformation brings more people and more money into the online world.

The music industry was the early leader in complaints of online piracy. New technology spread quickly among young people, and file sharing became so common on college campuses that academic officials had to create their own policies and safeguards to avoid lawsuits.

Moviemakers have also been vocal in their efforts to bring piracy issues to the forefront of the discussion around digital economics. The Motion Picture Association of America (MPAA) estimates that $6.1 billion a year is lost to piracy. In a study conducted for the association by LEK Consulting, global piracy revealed that losses were 75% greater than those sustained on hard goods. The lost dollars stem from lost ticket sales and lost DVD sales. While the problem is severe in countries such as China and Russia, it is not simply a foreign issue. Losses from U.S. piracy alone are estimated at $1.3 billion.[9]

The magnitude of the piracy problem is so great that the LEK study was delayed in its release while the MPAA conducted talks with its membership over the staggering problem and the necessary industry response.

When the study did surface, MPAA chairman and CEO Dan Glickman made a key point that has resonance for the greater community of digital transformation players:

> "The film industry is a thriving economic engine that generates jobs and exports in countries all over the world. We are calling on governments internationally to continue to work with us in limiting the impact of piracy on local economies and the film industry. Movies are a valuable product and intellectual property must be respected."[10]

Taken one step further, Glickman's comments have impact in the ad/marketing world as well. Why do consumers come to the Internet or to any other digital platform? It's for the content. We may produce the best, most alluring, most engaging advertising ever known, but if it is not alongside similarly gripping content, it will never produce results. Consumers come online for news, information, and entertainment. They log on day after day in search of what is new and engaging. If content online ceases to be either of those things, consumers will look elsewhere in a heartbeat. Today's consumers have no loyalty to any one device—be it new or old media. Consumers follow great content to any platform handy.

That being the case, piracy is everyone's problem. The movie producers may lose the $6.1 billion, the music industry may miss its $5 billion, and other publishers from comics to encyclopedias may suffer similar fates. Their problems are our problems because if the piracy issue is not resolved to their satisfaction, it is possible that they will simply move off the digital stage. Even a small pullback could be harmful. Consumers insist on the latest and greatest content. If they think they are getting watered-down versions of what the media giants have to offer, they will be less engaged, less eager to log on. That means fewer eyeballs online and a direct hit to the digital advertising industry.

The safety of online content is a core issue for anyone who hopes to make a living off the digitally transformed consumer conversation. As more consumers come online in search of the best possible entertainment experience, more content providers will be pressed into service. The advertising community needs them and must support their efforts to protect their wares. This requires attention to domestic piracy prevention and to the problem in the global marketplace. In today's connected economy, it is useless to crack down on misbehavior at home when the violators can simply move their operations to another country and continue with their business as usual. The response to piracy must involve local and international efforts. As daunting as that may sound, it is a critical issue. A lack of attention to the piracy issue could result in a vast wide digital space on which there is nothing of interest.

REGULATORY OVERKILL

What happens when a popular communications medium gets politicized? What is the result when commercial interests knock up against the political? No need to look to the digital technologies for an example. A prime case study in what happens when media meet politics took place over the radio airwaves in the case of controversial personality Howard Stern.

Stern's unique brand of provocative content was a staple on radio for years. He drew legions of regular listeners to his show and over the years rose to full-fledged celebrity status. But his fans were not the only ones listening. In recent years, Stern drew the attention of radio regulators—the Federal Communications Commission (FCC). Exercising their power as arbiters of the public interest, FCC regulators found that Stern's work had crossed the lines of public acceptability. Clean up the act, he was told, or get off the air.

The legal battle raged on for several years, with Stern slapped with fines. Finally, rather than alter his content, Stern opted to leave regular radio for the yet-unregulated world of satellite radio. Now, to hear his daily rants on everything from politics to sex to celebrity gossip, listeners must pay a monthly service fee to a satellite radio provider. The FCC was unable to remove Stern's content from the media mix, but it was able to hem it in. Experts say that while Stern's show remains viable, it has lost many listeners now that it has moved from ad-sponsored to paid status.

Why is this story relevant? It is a classic example of the ability of public interests to affect the scope of media. Players interested in capitalizing on the digital transformation will need to keep a close watch on Washington and how legislators and regulators are reacting to the changing technological landscape. As Stern learned, regulators can wield significant power over communications formats.

In the darker future of digital transformation, conflict between regulators and commercial interests could result in a framework of laws that undermine the ability of marketers and commerce to function.

WHAT TO WATCH FOR

Limits on advertising volume: One way regulators or legislators might try to tap into the digital advertising world is by attempting to block or set limits on the volume of advertising sent to consumers. Clearly, consumers are not shy about calling their congresspersons when ad volume reaches a tipping point. Already, the zealousness of e-mail marketers has created legislation such as the CAN-SPAM Act of 2003 (Controlling the Assault of Non-Solicited Pornography and Marketing Act). As more marketers tap into digital advertising, using tools such as e-mail, search, text messaging, and RSS, our industry will need to be aware of Washington's mood. A rise in complaints by consumers would result in other legislation restricting digital marketing. Certainly, the precedent for this kind of legislation exists.

Limits on advertising content: What is and is not acceptable content in a digital ad? Are there standards to be set for e-mail ads versus text messaging ads versus those triggered by a search engine? This discussion is likely to crop up around the topic of young people on the Internet. Parents may object to the products and services their kids can learn about simply by clicking through links and other invitations. On the one hand, the industry wouldn't want regulators to step in as copy editors. On the other hand, if visitors to MySpace.com can trigger ad content of a sexual nature, complaints will surely arise.

Requiring filters: While many access the Internet through privately owned technology, more and more public institutions are getting into the market. Millions of students access the Internet through schools or libraries. Increasingly, cities are equipping open public spaces with Wi-Fi, allowing anyone with a computer free access online. As the public sector gets into the role of Internet access provider, there will be more pressure on these public bodies to act as gatekeepers. Conceivably, this could lead to more aggressive filters—not just those that scan for objectionable material such as sexual content but also those that block out advertising content.

The response to these concerns must be proactive rather than reactive. The history of the relationship between Washington and media has long been one of regulatory debate. The economic success of the digital transformation rests on the free flow of ideas and commerce across these newly developed platforms. Standards of ethics and behavior are certainly important. They will provide us with guidelines and ethical constructs in which to navigate the new marketplace. Advertising without regulation opens the industry to criticism and steps away from our responsibilities as ethical businesspeople. It is not reasonable to deliver any ad to anyone at any time simply because a client will pay for it. Just as we live by ethical rules in traditional media, we must live by them in the digital marketplace as well.

But these standards need to originate from inside the industry. Waiting for Washington to create them will likely leave both consumers and marketers unhappy. It is not uncommon for the legislators charged with monitoring new technology to have only the earliest grasp of its use and potential. That can lead to legislation crafted around political themes rather than technological or economic realities. The best course for the industry will be to come up with guidelines that address these issues: volume, content, and public access. If we do not, it is certain that other forces will do it for us.

This work of self-regulation can pay off for an industry. Consider the efforts of the motion picture industry. Hoping to avoid government regulation of what's available on the big screen, the industry crafted its own set of guidelines. The rules were created and are governed by the industry association, MPAA. While creative players may complain about the rating they receive, overall, the system has worked. It protects consumers by creating a framework of ethical standards and behaviors for the industry. It protects the industry by creating a body of regulation and holding off outside regulators from exerting their own form of control.

The purpose of this chapter is not to throw cold water on the rise of digital advertising. It is rather to remind us all that while many good things can come of change, many unwanted circumstances can also arise. The key to staying out of what I call the dark side of digital transformation is to stay ahead of the potential pitfalls. We can learn from the media formats that have come before digital. We can see how those industries—radio, motion pictures, and television—have dealt with regulatory pressures and consumer backlash. We can get ahead of these concerns and can tap our own trade associations and industry leaders to help us come up with guidelines that protect against unnecessary roadblocks to digital success. Standards will evolve, with or without our input. Clearly, it is in our best interest to be there first.

FINAL THOUGHTS

Where do we go from here?

We began this conversation with a story about an aircraft carrier and a lighthouse ahead. It's a good story for a speech—it always gets a laugh. But the message to our industry is no laughing matter. For certain, like the aircraft carrier in the coastal waters, we must change course. We must leave off arguing with the change agents around us. Our insistence that the other guys change their course to get out of our way is not getting us where we need to be.

This is no longer a theoretical discussion for the advertising industry. It is a real moment of decision and one that does not offer unlimited time for pondering. Already, budgets are wandering. Companies are wondering whether advertising is the best route to consumers today. The money is migrating to other industries. This is not a problem staked out some time in the future—it is a current hurdle. The lighthouse manager in the anecdote delivers the punch line when he tells the captain of the oncoming vessel: your call. But of course there is no choice in the matter. Not for the captain in the story, not for our industry in the digital transformation. Change must happen. It is simply now a matter of whether we make this change in a timely fashion or whether we wait until we've run aground to accept our situation.

Still, change for change's sake will not help us navigate the transformation. We must embrace change with purpose. We must set our course based on what we know is changing around us.

We are not making this journey in a vacuum. There are signs around us that point us in the right direction.

We must embrace empowered consumers. We must learn to share control of advertising information. Consumers are no longer our passive audience. The viewers who once waited eagerly for the next serving of information and entertainment have been left in the dust by the lean-forward generation. These new consumers are running their own show, and they have no taste for waiting. They don't even wait for the seconds it takes a Web page to load, much less for the time a marketer might want to ascertain a trend. They are engaged in getting what they want when they want it. But their reach for the controls is not an altogether harmful event. Indeed, they have said to us that they want to participate in the process. We cannot hope to hold them back. We must bring them in, setting a shared course through the new digital advertising world.

We must embrace new technologies. We must reach out to test and build skills with what is new to the market. We must bring in the talent and vision that will spot new technology in the pipeline. We must reach out to the industries that are dreaming up the great new ideas and convince them to join with us and leverage this newness in the furtherance of marketing goals. Resisting the new technologies because they seem expensive or untested simply sends them elsewhere. It does not lessen their impact on our industry. Instead, it sends them into the arms of others that will eventually use them to chip away at our position in the commercial world. To remain relevant, to remain the central creative force in advertising and marketing, we must make technology a core competency of our industry.

We must be willing to abandon traditions. While it once worked to divide our efforts into device-oriented silos, we must be willing to recognize how this construct has shifted. This does not denigrate how things were once done, but it recognizes that no one system lasts forever. Thinking of our efforts in their most elemental terms—text, audio, and video—will help us to see that the device is not the most important aspect of advertising. It is simply the platform of the moment. We must be willing to move on from old concepts of how this business must be organized.

We must recognize the new speed of the universe. The impetus to sit on the sidelines and wait until a clear course ahead emerges is a recipe for disaster. While "wait and see" might have been a smart route in the days when change happened over years, even generations, today it is outdated advice. The companies and industries that wait and see will see their futures move ahead without them. Consumers are moving ahead. We cannot afford to wait and see—they have already left. Not only must we catch up, but also we must find ways to recapture the first-mover advantage in the marketer-consumer relationship. To do that, we must be out in front of the consumers, not waiting to see how change plays out.

This is not a debate over tactics. We are not engaged in a debate over whether the 30-second spot is dead or whether search should get more of less of a client's budget. We have had a broader conversation about where we are as an industry and what has led us to this point and what events have shaped us. We are now at the point where we must take a proactive stance in our own history. We must be ready to lead, not just with our advice but with our products and in the way we run our companies. We must be ready to do more than just function in the era of digital transformation. We must recognize our ability and our mandate to be leaders.

Ultimately, what we decide to do as an industry will have broad societal impact. We are the industry that influences. We are the crafters of what is desirable, what is worthwhile, and what we hope to acquire and accomplish in our lives. How we manage change will be watched and reviewed. Whether we hold our position as influencers will be determined. Are we still the industry spotting the trends and leading marketing to its connection to consumers?

It's your call.

Notes

Chapter 1: The New Normal

1. Alvin Toffler, *Future Shock* (New York: Random House, 1970).
2. David Schatsky, "The Fragmented Media Future," Jupiter Research analyst weblog, January 4, 2006.
3. Ithiel de Sola Pool, *Technologies of Freedom* (Cambridge, MA: The Belknap Press of Harvard University Press, 1983), 27, 28.
4. Alan Moore, "Into the Darknet," Communities Dominate Brands weblog, August 12, 2005.
5. Vinton Cerf, speech to Maine Telecommunications Users Group, February 2004.

Chapter 2: The Way We Were

1. H. G. Wells, *In the Days of the Comet* (New York: Century, 1906), Book 1, "The Comet," Chapter 1, "Dust in the Shadows."
2. William L. Bird, Jr., *Better Living* (Chicago: Northwestern University Press, 1999), Chapter 4.
3. Waldemar Kaempffert, "Who Will Pay For Broadcasting?" *Popular Radio*, December 1922, 236.
4. Thomas H. White, "United States Early Radio History," http://earlyradiohistory.us/.
5. J. C. McQuiston, "Advertising by Radio: Can and Should It Be Done?" *Radio News*, August 1922, 232.
6. Thomas H. White, "United States Early Radio History," http://earlyradiohistory.us/.
7. Ibid.
8. Ibid.

9. William L. Bird, Jr., *Better Living* (Chicago: Northwestern University Press, 1999), Chapter 4.
10. "The 75 Biggest Moments of the Advertising Age," *Advertising Age*, March 28, 2005.
11. Michael Ritchie, *Please Stand By: A Prehistory of Television* (Woodstock, NY: Overlook, 1994).
12. Ibid.
13. Lawrence R. Samuel, *Brought to You By: Postwar Television Advertising and the American Dream* (Austin: University of Texas Press, 2001), Chapter 1.
14. Ibid.
15. *Editor & Publisher Yearbook*, online data, 1940-2003, www.editorandpublisher.com
16. Lawrence R. Samuel, *Brought to You By: Postwar Television Advertising and the American Dream* (Austin: University of Texas Press, 2001), Chapter 1.
17. Sharon Strover, *The Encyclopedia of Television*, First Edition. Editor: Horace Newcomb, Publisher: Fitzroy Dearborn Publishers 1997 as on Chicago Museum Of Broadcast Communications Web site: http://www.museum.tv/archives/etv/U/htmlU/unitedstatesc/unitedstatesc.htm
18. *TV Guide* poll, May 1979.
19. "The 75 Biggest Moments of the Advertising Age," *Advertising Age*, March 28, 2005, 56.

Chapter 3: Where We Are Today

1. David Schatsky, "The Fragmented Media Future," Jupiter Research analyst weblog, January 4, 2006.
2. Toyota press release, April 24, 2006.
3. IBM Business Consulting Services, *The End of Television as We Know It: A Future Industry Perspective* (IBM Institute for Business Value, March 27, 2006).
4. "Portable Media Players: Competing in an Evolving Marketplace," Jupiter Research, August 2005.
5. Ibid.

6. Anthony J. Hopp, "The Power and the Magic," speech at 2006 American Association of Advertising Agencies Management Conference for Agency CEOs, April 2006.

Chapter 4: The Three Futures of Advertising

1. Robert Frost, "The Road Not Taken," *Mountain Interval* (New York: Holt, 1916).

Chapter 5: The Empowered Consumer

1. Anonymous posting, http://www.washingtonmonthly.com/mt/mt-comments.cgi?entry_id=3765.
2. Steve Rubel, "Building Word of Mouth through Community Marketing," speech at iMedia Brand Summit, March 2005.
3. Alan Lightman, *Einstein's Dreams* (New York: Warner, 1994), 126.
4. Barry Schwartz, *The Paradox of Choice* (New York: Harper Collins, 2004), prologue.
5. Simultaneous Media Survey, BIGresearch, August 10, 2006.
6. Tim Armstrong, "The Flip Side of Fear," *The American Society of Information, Science and Technology Bulletin*, December/January 2006.

Chapter 6: Advertising and Politics

1. TNS Media Intelligence/Campaign Media Analysis Group, December 31, 2005.
2. Ibid.
3. Ibid.
4. Jon Gertner, "The Very, Very Personal Is the Political," *The New York Times*, February 15, 2004.
5. 2005 Digital Future Report, Center for the Digital Future, University of Southern California Annenberg School.
6. Ibid.
7. TNS Media Intelligence/Campaign Media Analysis Group, 2005.
8. Rick Klein, "Democratic Group Targets Senate GOP," *The Boston Globe*, March 2, 2006.

9. TNS Media Intelligence/Campaign Media Analysis Group, 2005.
10. Ibid.
11. Ibid.
12. Shankar Gupta, "Consultants: Politicos Coming Around on Online Ads," MediaPost Publications, May 17, 2005.
13. Justin Oberman, "Hola! Mobile Voter," *Personal Democracy Forum*, July 21, 2006.
14. 2005 Digital Future Report, Center for the Digital Future, University of Southern California Annenberg School.

Chapter 7: The Future of Agencies

1. Digital Media Trends survey, American Advertising Federation, June 11, 2006.
2. David Hallerman, "Online Video Advertising: Promises and Challenges," December 2005.
3. Burst Media Research, May 2006.
4. Ibid.
5. Diego Vasquez, "With Teens, the Web Is, like Addicting," *Media Life Magazine*, June 13, 2006.
6. "Move along the Marketing Accountability Curve," July 20, 2005, presentation at Association of National Advertisers 2005 Marketing Accountability Forum.
7. Jean Halliday, "Chrysler Exits Arnell, Haggles over BBDO Pact; Architect of Celine Deal out after Chanteuse Spots Fall Flat," *Advertising Age*, December 8, 2003.

Chapter 8: Digital Transformation and Vertical Industries

1. The Keynote Customer Experience (CE) Rankings for the Third Party Auto Industry, Keynote Systems, March 23, 2005.
2. Polk Center for Automotive Studies, "Building the Pipeline: Insights on First-Time Buyers," 2006.
3. "Research Alert," Jupiter Research, December 16, 2005.
4. Bill Nussey, "The Digital Marketer," *Silverpop*, June 2006.
5. Ellen Neuborne, "May I Help You?" *Inc. Magazine*, January 2006.
6. TNS Media Intelligence, 2001–2005.

7. 2005 Digital Future Report, Center for the Digital Future, University of Southern California Annenberg School.
8. ComScore, Movie Advertising Case Study, Integrate '06 Summit.
9. Outsell, February 2006.
10. TNS Media Intelligence, 2001–2005.
11. Ellen Neuborne, "Scooby-Doo, Where Aren't You?" Businessweek.com, May 2002.
12. TNS Media Intelligence, 2001–2005.
13. Ibid.
14. Harley Manning, "Make the Most of Your Financial Services Brand on the Web," Forrest Research, May 16, 2006.
15. Ibid.
16. Transcript of speech by Edwin L. Artzt, CEO of Procter and Gamble, to the American Association of Advertising Agencies Conference, *Advertising Age*, May 23, 1994.
17. Jason Gertzen, "Kraft Surprise to Find Ad On Racist Web Site," *The Milwaukee Journal Sentinel*, January 8, 2005.
18. Tamara Mendelsohn, "Differentiating the Grocery Experience," Forrester Research, June 19, 2006.
19. TNS Media Intelligence, 2001–2005.
20. Transcript of speech by Edwin L. Artzt, CEO of Procter and Gamble, to the American Association of Advertising Agencies Conference, *Advertising Age*, May 23, 1994.
21. TNS Media Intelligence, 2001–2005.
22. Ibid.
23. Bradford J. Holmes, "Topic Overview: Consumer Marketing in Healthcare," Forrester Research, June 15, 2006.

Chapter 9: Law and Order

1. Susannah Fox, "Spyware Problems Have Struck Tens of Millions of Computer Users," Pew Internet and American Life Project, July 6, 2005.
2. Ibid.
3. Association of National Advertisers 2005 Compendium of Legislative, Regulatory and Legal Issues.

4. Eric Goldman, "Data Mining and Attention Consumption," 2005.
5. Elinor Mills, "Google Click Fraud Settlement Given Go-Ahead," CNET News.com, ZDNet News, July 27, 2006.
6. "Hot Topics: Click Fraud Reaches $1.3 Billion, Dictates End of 'Don't Ask, Don't Tell' Era," Outsell, June 29, 2006.
7. Ibid.
8. Ibid.
9. Brian Quinton, "Click Fraud Has Radiator.com Boiling," *Direct*, June 15, 2006.
10. AIT press release, December 8, 2005.
11. Ed Oswald, "Google Tests Cost-Per-Action Ads," BetaNews, June 22, 2006.
12. Eric Goldman, Technology and Law blog, http://blog.ericgoldman.org/archives/search_engines/.
13. http://www.techdirt.com/articles/20060607/0334227.shtml.

Chapter 10: The Potential Dark Side

1. "Review of Issues Related to the Loss of VA Information Involving the Identity of Millions of Veterans, Department of Veterans Affairs," Office of Inspector General, July 11, 2006.
2. Ibid.
3. Declan McCullagh, "Police Blotter: Wells Fargo not Required to Encrypt Data," CNET News.com, April 14, 2006.
4. Dawn Kawamoto, "Illinois University Hit with Security Breach," CNET News.com, July 6, 2006.
5. Susanna Fox, "Spyware Problems Have Struck Tens of Millions of Computer Users," Pew Internet and American Life Project, July 6, 2005.
6. Ibid.
7. Abbey Klassen, "How to Build a Video on Demand Ad," *Advertising Age*, July 17, 2006.
8. Jack Neff, "J&J Pioneers New Marketing Rules," *Advertising Age*, May 22, 2006.
9. 2005 Piracy Data Summary, Motion Picture Association of America.
10. Motion Picture Association of America, May 3, 2006.